I0096664

You Weren't Supposed to Know This

Surviving Bureaucracy, Dodging Pitfalls, and Getting What You Need Without Losing Your Mind

James Ergle

Copyright © 2025 by James Ergle

All rights reserved.

This work is licensed under a Creative Commons Attribution–NonCommercial 4.0 International License (CC BY-NC 4.0).

You are free to copy, distribute, adapt, and share this work for any non-commercial purpose, provided proper attribution is given.

Commercial use, resale, or publication in for-profit formats requires express written permission from the author.

To view a copy of this license, visit creativecommons.org/licenses/by-nc/4.0.

This book is independently published by the author. Cover design and interior layout by the author.

Printed and distributed via IngramSpark (paperback). Ebook and print edition available through Amazon Kindle.

For more work by the author, visit:
https://radicalleanings.substack.com

First edition: 2025

ISBN: 978-1-969636-00-4

A Personal Note Before You Begin

This book was written for people who were never supposed to figure it out.

You weren't meant to know how to push back, how to appeal, how to get through the maze without giving up. You were meant to be tired, isolated, and ashamed. That's how the system keeps working—by making sure most people never see how it actually functions.

This is not a feel-good book. It's a weapon. A manual. A way out of some of the traps you were never warned about.

If you're holding it, it means you're either in the fight already or about to be. You might be broke, evicted, working three jobs, raising kids on your own, sitting in jail, helping someone inside, or just tired of being lied to. Or maybe you're the one who always steps in when others fall. Either way, this is for you.

Everything in here is legal to share. There's no paywall. No affiliate links. No bait. If it helps someone you love, copy it. Print it. Send it. I don't care if I ever get credit. I care that you make it.

Thank you for giving this your time. I hope it gives you something back.

—Jim

Table of Contents

Introduction

Why This Book Exists

If you've picked this up, you probably already know something's broken. Not just in the abstract, but in the day-to-day grind of trying to get anything done when you're poor, sick, undocumented, disabled, overworked, or just unlucky.

You've tried to apply for help, file the right forms, call the right number. You've waited on hold, been transferred, been told to fax something in 2025. You've read the website five times and still don't know what they want. You've wondered if it's just you.

It's not.

This book isn't about theory. It's not about changing the system. It's about surviving it. It's a field guide for the people who have to make it through anyway—people like you, or someone you love.

What's inside are practical tactics for navigating bureaucracies that are hostile by design. It won't make you an expert in tax law or disability claims or prison policy. But it *will* show you how to hold your ground, push back effectively, and spot the traps they don't warn you about.

There are no magic words. No guaranteed scripts. But there *is* a pattern to the bullshit. Once you see it, you can start to move differently. Not perfectly. Just better.

You weren't supposed to know this. That's why it matters that you do.

Chapter 1: How to Get Food, Rent Help, and Medicaid Without Giving Up

The system often feels like it is built to make you quit.

You fill out forms, wait on hold, get told to try again and then they hope you give up. Whether you are applying for food assistance, cash help, rent money, or healthcare, the process is slow, frustrating, and full of traps. That is not your fault. It is how the system limits who gets help.

But if you know how the game works, you can stay in it long enough to win.

SNAP: The Food Help You Are Entitled To

What SNAP Is:
The Supplemental Nutrition Assistance Program (SNAP), known as food stamps, gives monthly grocery money on an EBT card (Electronic Benefits Transfer). The card works like a debit card at most grocery stores and markets that accept SNAP.

Who Qualifies:

- You may qualify if your household income is below about 130% of the federal poverty line.

    - For one person in 2025, that is about **$19,600 per year**.

    - For a family of three, it is around **$33,300 per year**.

- Some states count **gross income** (before taxes), others use

net income (after deductions).

- Some states have asset limits, usually $2,750 in countable assets (bank accounts, cash), or $4,250 if someone in the home is over 60 or disabled.

If You Are Homeless:
You can still qualify. You may use a friend's address, a shelter's mailing address, or a community center that agrees to accept mail for you.

How to Apply:

- Visit your state's SNAP office or website.

- Many states allow online applications and digital uploads of documents.

- You can check for your state's program at **Benefits.gov** or by searching "[your state] SNAP application."

Program Names Change by State:
SNAP is called **CalFresh** in California, **FoodShare** in Wisconsin, and **Lone Star Card** in Texas. When in doubt, check your state's official website.

Follow Up:
Check your application status weekly through online portals or by calling. Delays are common.

TANF: Cash Help for Families with Children

What TANF Is:
Temporary Assistance for Needy Families (TANF) provides cash aid to families with children. It is harder to get than SNAP because of strict income limits, asset rules, work requirements,

and lifetime limits.

Who Qualifies:

- You need to have a dependent child or be pregnant.

- You usually must meet strict income guidelines.

- Most states require you to participate in work activities. This may include job searches, training, volunteering, or education programs.

- Some states give exemptions for parents of very young children, pregnant women, or people with disabilities.

How Much You Get:

- TANF amounts vary widely.

  - About **$450 per month** for a family of three in California.

  - As low as **$170 per month** in Mississippi.

Time Limits:

- The federal limit is **60 months (5 years) total over your lifetime**.

- Some states have shorter limits, like **24 or 36 months**.

- Some states allow hardship extensions.

How to Apply:

- Usually through your local **Department of Human Services**.

- TANF often requires an in-person interview or caseworker appointment.

Emergency Assistance: One-Time Help You May Have to Hunt For

What It Is:
Emergency assistance is a general term for help with rent, utilities, or eviction notices. It often comes from local charities, churches, nonprofits, or county programs. These funds are rarely advertised, and you usually have to ask directly.

Where to Look:

- **LIHEAP (Low-Income Home Energy Assistance Program):** Helps with heating and cooling bills. Apply through state energy offices or local community action agencies.

- **Emergency Rental Assistance (ERA):** Some local governments still offer these programs, even though most COVID-era federal funding ended.

- **Local 211:** Call **211** or visit **211.org** to find nonprofits, housing programs, and community aid in your area. Speaking to a live operator often works better than browsing the website.

- **Charities:** Groups like **Catholic Charities**, **Salvation Army**, or **Jewish Family Services** often offer help, even if you are not a member.

What You'll Need:

- ID and proof of address

- Proof of the emergency (like an eviction notice or utility shutoff notice)

- Proof of income or a statement of no income

Medicaid: Health Coverage That Fights to Kick You Off

What Medicaid Is:
Medicaid is a health insurance program for people with low incomes. It covers doctor visits, prescriptions, hospital care, and more, often with no cost or very low co-pays.

Who Qualifies:
- In **Medicaid expansion states** (41 states plus D.C. as of 2025), you may qualify if your income is below **138% of the federal poverty line** (around **$20,800 per year** for one person).

- In **non-expansion states** (like Alabama, Texas, Florida), the rules are stricter, usually limited to parents, pregnant women, or people with disabilities.

- Check **Healthcare.gov** or your state's Medicaid website for details.

Emergency Medicaid:
- Covers life-threatening emergencies or childbirth.

- Often available to undocumented immigrants or people who do not qualify for regular Medicaid.

Charity Care:
- Nonprofit hospitals are required by federal law to offer financial help (called charity care).

- You must ask for it and provide proof of income.

- Contact the hospital's billing department to apply.

How to Apply:

- Online through your state's Medicaid portal or **Healthcare.gov**.

- If denied, ask for the reason in writing and appeal within the deadline (usually **60–90 days**).

Program Names Change by State:
Medicaid may be called **MassHealth** in Massachusetts or **Medi-Cal** in California.

Follow Up:
Check your application status weekly. The system will not update you unless you chase it.

How They Stall You And How You Fight Back

Stall Tactic	What To Do
"We did not get your documents."	Keep scanned copies. Use email, online portals, or fax with confirmation.
"The system is down today."	Ask for a receipt or proof you showed up.
"You need to call back."	Write down names, dates, and ask for a supervisor.
"That program is closed."	Ask when it closed and if there is a replacement program.
"We cannot help you here."	Ask who can help and request a direct transfer or name.

Appeals: What You Need to Know

- If you are denied, appeal immediately.

- **SNAP appeals:** You usually have **90 days**.

- **Medicaid appeals: 60–90 days** depending on state rules.

- **TANF appeals:** Vary by state, sometimes as short as **30 days.** Check the denial letter.

Fair Hearings:

- A formal process where you can present your case to a judge.

- Bring your documents, a timeline of events, and a written summary of the problem.

- You have the right to explain your side and show evidence.

Get Legal Help If You Can:

- Find free or low-cost legal aid at **www.lsc.gov/find-legal-aid**.

- Many Legal Aid groups will help with appeals for SNAP, TANF, or Medicaid.

How to Build a Paper Trail That Keeps You Safe

- **Always keep copies** of applications, letters, and submitted documents.

- **Use email or online portals** when you can, so you have confirmation receipts.

- **Take notes** on every call of who you spoke to, when, and what they said.

- **Use a free email account** (like Gmail) just for government paperwork.

- **Scan documents with your phone** using apps like Adobe

Scan or CamScanner.

If You Are Homeless:
A signed letter from a friend, shelter, or community group can count as proof of address.

Community Support:

- **Libraries** often offer free internet, printers, scanners, and even help from staff.

- **Community centers, churches, and shelters** may have people who can guide you.

- Some areas have **nonprofits or legal aid clinics** that offer benefits workshops or help with applications.

Watch Out for Scams

- **You do not have to pay** for help with SNAP, TANF, or Medicaid.

- Applications and help are always free.

- Only apply through trusted sites like **Benefits.gov**, **Healthcare.gov**, or your state's official portals.

- If someone offers "guaranteed approval" for a fee, it is a scam.

Final Word

You deserve help. You are not lazy, and you are not asking for a handout.

The system is confusing on purpose. It is slow on purpose. It hopes you will give up.

Do not.

Keep your copies. Know your deadlines. File your appeals.

If you push back, you have a real chance. And you are not alone in the fight.

Chapter 2: How to Actually Get Your Social Security Retirement Check

One System That Mostly Works Because the Rich Use It Too

Social Security retirement is one of the rare systems in America that doesn't seem designed to humiliate you or make you quit halfway through. That's not because the government suddenly grew a heart. It's because retirees vote, retirees sue, and rich people with pensions and stock dividends also file for it.

So the system, while bloated and sometimes glitchy, mostly works.

Here's how to make sure you get what you're owed with as little hassle as possible.

Who Qualifies

You qualify for Social Security retirement if:

- You've worked enough years to earn **40 credits** (that's about 10 years of work, but it depends on income per year).

- You've reached age **62** or older.

Unlike SSI or SSDI, retirement Social Security doesn't care if you're broke, rich, sick, or healthy. If you've paid in, you're eligible.

When You Can Get It And What Changes If You Wait

- **62**: You can claim early benefits starting at age 62 but they'll be reduced by up to 30% compared to your full benefit.

- **Full Retirement Age (FRA)**: Between **66 and 67**, depending on your birth year. You'll get your full benefit here.

- **70**: If you delay until 70, your monthly benefit will be the highest it can be, thanks to delayed retirement credits.

Waiting longer = higher monthly check. But you don't have to wait if you need the money now.

How to Apply

- **Online** at SSA.gov is the easiest and fastest.

- **By phone** at 1-800-772-1213.

- **In person** at a local SSA office (by appointment recommended).

What you'll need:

- Your Social Security number.

- Birth certificate.

- Work history.

- Bank account info for direct deposit.

- Marriage or divorce papers (if they affect your benefits).

They don't make this part hard because they want the process clean for everyone.

How Much Will You Get?

- Based on your **35 highest-earning years**.

- Adjusted for inflation.

- Reduced if you claim early.

You can check your estimated benefit by creating a **My Social Security** account at SSA.gov.

Cost of Living Adjustments (COLA)

Unlike most government help, Social Security gets adjusted almost every year for inflation. That's the **COLA** — Cost of Living Adjustment.

It's automatic. You don't have to ask for it.

How They Can Screw You And How to Avoid It

Even a working system has flaws. Here's where people get caught:

- **Overpayments**: If SSA sends you too much (it happens), they'll claw it back. Always read your benefit notices.

- **Missing paperwork**: If they request something (like proof of marriage) and you ignore it, your check can be delayed.

- **Banking errors**: Make sure your direct deposit info is right. SSA doesn't cover bank screw-ups.

Pro tip: Set a calendar reminder once a year to log into SSA.gov and check your info.

Spousal and Survivor Benefits

- You may qualify for benefits based on a spouse's work record.

- Widows and widowers may get survivor benefits.

- Divorced spouses (if married 10+ years) can also qualify.

This system is often overlooked and it's worth checking.

Final Word

SSA retirement is about as close as America gets to a functional benefit. It's not charity. You paid for it.

Unlike most of the traps in this book, this one's real and it's yours if you claim it. Just don't forget to apply.

Chapter 3: Disability and SSI And How It Actually Works

The Application You're Supposed to Fail

The disability system is a trap. Not a safety net but a trap. It is packed with rules they never explain, timelines they do not follow, and questions designed to make you feel like a liar. That is not by mistake. The system works by discouragement.

About two out of three people get denied the first time they apply for disability. That does not mean you do not qualify. It means you walked into a bureaucracy that was never designed to help you.

This chapter breaks down the difference between **SSI** and **SSDI**, how the process really works, and what they hope you never figure out.

SSI vs. SSDI: What's the Difference?

These programs sound similar but work differently:

- **SSDI (Social Security Disability Insurance):**
    - For people who worked enough years in jobs that paid Social Security taxes.
    - Requires **40 work credits**, with **20 earned in the last 10 years** before your disability began. Younger workers may need fewer credits.
    - Based on your past income.
    - Benefit amounts typically range from **$1,500 to**

$3,000 per month.

- **SSI (Supplemental Security Income):**
  - For people with low or no income and limited work history.
  - Strict income limits of around **$914 per month** for individuals in **2025**, with certain deductions allowed (like $20 general income and $65 of earned income).
  - Maximum payment is **$943 per month for individuals** and **$1,415 for couples** in 2025.
- **Dual Eligibility:** You may qualify for both if you meet SSDI work requirements and SSI's strict income and asset limits — often applying to low-income disabled workers. SSI asset limits are **$2,000 for individuals** and **$3,000 for couples**.

The application form simply asks, "Do you want to apply for disability?" Say yes. They will figure out which program fits.

The Application Gauntlet

You can apply online at **SSA.gov**, by phone, or in person at a Social Security office. Expect delays and be prepared for skepticism.

What You Will Need:

- Medical records from licensed providers, showing diagnoses, test results (like MRIs), treatment notes, and evaluations.

- A statement explaining how your condition prevents full-time work.

- Dates, diagnoses, and documented attempts at treatment, even if they did not help.

- Non-medical evidence like statements from family, friends, or employers can help support your case.

They look for three things:

1. **A Named Condition:** "Back pain" is not enough. "Degenerative disc disease" might be.

2. **Functional Limitations:** Examples include inability to focus for more than 10 minutes, panic attacks preventing regular work, or inability to follow instructions due to schizophrenia.

3. **Evidence:** Clinic notes, hospital records, doctor letters, psychiatric evaluations, therapy notes, medication records.

Decisions typically take **3–6 months**. Severe cases may qualify for expedited processing under SSA's **Compassionate Allowances Program**.

Start Early: Filing starts your protective filing date, which helps preserve backpay eligibility.

Application Support: SSA's **Disability Starter Kit** at **ssa.gov/disability/disability_starter_kits.htm** provides free templates.

What They Mean by "Substantial Gainful Activity"

They do not just care if you are sick. They care if you can still produce value.

Substantial Gainful Activity (SGA):

- Can you earn more than **$1,550 per month in 2025** from work? For blind individuals, the limit is **$2,590**.

- Only earned income counts — not pensions or gifts.

- Income from special accommodations or subsidized wages may not count as SGA.

Failed work attempts can help your case if you document them. Trial Work Periods allow SSDI recipients to test work for **9 months** without losing benefits.

Mental Illness and the Invisible Wall

Mental health conditions like anxiety, PTSD, depression, bipolar disorder, autism, and schizophrenia are real disabilities but harder to prove without hospitalization.

How to Strengthen Your Case:

- Show a history of therapy, medication, or crisis care.

- Get detailed letters from licensed therapists or psychiatrists.

- Provide therapy notes, psychiatric evaluations, medication records, and crisis intervention reports.

- Keep symptom journals or statements from family/friends. These help but cannot replace medical records.

- Align your statements with your providers' records.

How to Survive a Denial (Because You Probably Will Be)

If denied, **do not start over. Appeal.**

- You have **60 days** to request reconsideration. Approval rates are around **10–15%**, but it keeps your case alive.

- If denied again, request a hearing with an **Administrative Law Judge (ALJ).** Approval rates here are around **45–50%**.

    - Hearings often take **12–24 months** to schedule.

    - You can request your case file through **SSA.gov** or by calling **1-800-772-1213**.

    - Prepare for vocational expert testimony about your ability to work any job.

    - Practice answers to questions like "How does your condition affect daily life?"

Backpay covers the time since your application date.

What Lawyers Do And What You Can Do Without One

Lawyers are not required but can help, especially at hearings.

- They work on contingency, taking **25% of your backpay**, capped at **$7,200 in 2025**, with SSA's approval.

- They help review your file, gather missing records, and prepare you for questions.

- Some offer free consultations.

Find Help:

19

- **NOSSCR.org** — Find experienced disability attorneys.

- **www.lsc.gov/find-legal-aid** — Free or low-cost legal aid.

- **DisabilityBenefitsCenter.org** — Free SSDI/SSI guides.

How People Get Cut Off After Approval (And How to Avoid It)

SSA reviews your case every **3 or 5–7 years**.

- **Every 3 years** if your condition may improve.

- **Every 5–7 years** for permanent or severe conditions.

Common Reasons for Losing Benefits:

- Earning too much money.

- Not returning your **Continuing Disability Review (CDR)** packet (Form **SSA-454**).

- Lack of recent medical records.

Protect Yourself:

- Report income honestly.

- Keep copies of review paperwork.

- Stay in treatment or check in with a doctor regularly.

If Cut Off:

- Appeal within **60 days**.

- Request within **10 days** if you want benefits to continue during the appeal.

Final Word

Disability is a right. It's not a favor.

If you cannot work consistently because of your condition, you deserve help to survive.

They will try to make you feel like a fraud. They are afraid of people like you getting approved.

Do not let shame make you quit.

Do not let bureaucracy wear you down.

You are not asking for special treatment. You are asking for a fair shot at staying alive.

Extra Help and Resources

- **SSA's Compassionate Allowances:** Fast-tracks severe cases at **ssa.gov/compassionateallowances**.

- **SSA's Ticket to Work Program:** Free job training with protection for your benefits at **ssa.gov/work**.

- **Medicaid/Medicare Links:**
    - SSI often comes with Medicaid.
    - SSDI includes Medicare after a **24-month waiting period**.

- **Community Help:** Community health clinics, Area Agencies on Aging — **eldercare.acl.gov** — can help with records and applications.

Technology Tips

- Use a free email account (like Gmail) to track SSA letters.

- Scan documents with apps like Adobe Scan.

- Log out of public computers to protect your information.

Cultural and Language Barriers

- Call **1-800-772-1213** for free interpreters.

- SSA.gov offers forms in Spanish and other languages.

- Libraries and community centers often help with translations or applications.

Mental Health and Motivation

- The process can feel humiliating, but your disability is real.

- Take one step at a time.

- Community health centers, libraries, or senior centers can help you get started.

Chapter 4: Federal, State, Local? Who Do I Even Ask?

The Three-Headed Beast

The government feels like one big system, but it is really three competing levels of **federal**, **state**, and **local**. They fight, overlap, and pass the buck. When agencies say "that's not us," it often means they are underfunded, overworked, narrowly assigned, or bound by strict program funding rules.

This chapter explains the federal, state, and local roles, why you get misdirected, and how to find the right office or escalate when stuck.

Follow the Funding Trail

Most programs start with federal money but pass through state and local layers before reaching you.

- The **federal government** creates programs like SNAP (funded by the USDA), Medicaid (HHS), and Housing Choice Vouchers (HUD). These agencies set rules but rarely interact directly with applicants.

- **State governments** control eligibility, set extra rules, and add restrictions. For example, SNAP is federally funded, but California or Texas set income limits and manage applications.

- **Local agencies** — usually counties or cities — handle applications, paperwork, and case management.

Example: SNAP is a federal benefit, but you apply through your

state's Department of Human Services (DHS). The USDA will refer you to your state. If your local office fails you, escalate to the state.

Medicaid Expansion Note: As of 2025, ten states have not expanded Medicaid. Non-expansion states (like Alabama, Florida, and Texas) often limit Medicaid to parents, pregnant women, or disabled adults with incomes below **40–100% of the federal poverty line** (about **$6,000 to $15,060 annually**).

Some counties outsource services to private agencies. These agencies must follow federal and state rules but may have inconsistent processes. Verify their authority with your state agency.

Navigating Local Systems and Hidden Resources

County Challenges: Some counties make applications harder on purpose, especially in non-expansion states.

- Always ask, "Do you have a local advocate or ombudsman?" Ombudsmen vary by program (Medicaid, SNAP, long-term care) and can be found through state websites or **211**.

- If one caseworker stonewalls you, try calling another day.

- Check if your county offers online portals; some do, some do not.

- If services are contracted out, ask who funds them and check with the state for oversight.

Hidden Resources: Many offices help but do not advertise. Some are buried on outdated websites or serve specific groups.

- **Fair Housing Offices:** Handle housing discrimination under the Fair Housing Act, including issues like eviction or denial of housing based on disability or race. Find them at **hud.gov/program_offices/fair_housing_equal_opp**.

- **Legal Aid Clinics:** Offer free help with civil cases like evictions or benefits appeals. Prioritize low-income clients. Find services at **www.lsc.gov/find-legal-aid**.

- **Area Agencies on Aging:** Help seniors (60+) with Medicaid, SNAP, transportation, and local resources. Find them at **eldercare.acl.gov**.

- **County Health Navigators:** Assist with Medicaid, insurance, or healthcare access.

Call **211** to speak with a live operator who can locate local programs. Online directories like **Benefits.gov**, **USA.gov**, and **CommunityActionPartnership.com** help too.

How to Escalate

Escalation means moving up the chain with documents and facts, not yelling.

1. Ask for a supervisor.
2. Contact the state agency's complaint line or online complaint form.
3. Reach out to elected officials — county commissioner, city council, state legislator, or U.S. Representative (**Congress.gov** helps you find them).
4. Search for a state ombudsman specific to your program.

Your U.S. Representative can push SSA, HUD, or state agencies to review cases faster but they cannot approve or change eligibility decisions.

Escalation Works Best When You:

- Keep a written timeline.

- Stay calm, factual, and specific.

- Reference policy when possible.

- Keep digital copies of correspondence.

Quick Reference: Who Handles What?

Need	Contact First	Backup/Escalate
SNAP/Food Stamps	County DHS Office	State DHS, USDA Hotline (1-800-221-5689)
Medicaid	State Health Portal	Legal Aid, County Navigator
Rent Help	Local Housing Authority	City Council, HUD Regional Office (hud.gov/local)
Disability (SSI/SSDI)	Social Security Office (1-800-772-1213)	Legal Aid, Congressional Rep
Utility Shutoff	Local Assistance Agency	State Public Utility Commission (may offer shutoff protection)
Eviction	Local Court / Tenant Hotline (check with Legal Aid)	Legal Aid, Fair Housing Office

Examples You Can Use

- **SNAP Denial:** If denied, check eligibility on **Benefits.gov** and escalate to your state DHS.

- **Medicaid Delay:** Contact a County Health Navigator or state ombudsman through **211**.

- **Eviction Threat:** Call a tenant rights hotline (state-specific) or Fair Housing Office.

Scams Warning

Scammers may pose as government officials by phone or email.

- Never pay for benefits help.

- Use only official sites like **Benefits.gov**, **SSA.gov**, or state portals.

- Verify calls with SSA (**1-800-772-1213**) or USDA (**1-800-221-5689**).

Technology Tips

- Apply online when possible — check your state DHS site.

- Save confirmation emails and keep a "Benefits" folder.

- Use Adobe Scan or similar apps for documents.

- Log out of public computers.

- If no online portal exists, ask **211** or your state DHS about paper forms.

Cultural and Language Barriers

- Call **211** for interpreters.

- Many state DHS and SSA sites have forms in Spanish, Mandarin, and other languages.

- Libraries or community centers can help with translations or online applications.

Mental Health and Motivation

This process can wear you down. Take it one step at a time. Call one number. Visit one office. Community centers, churches, or nonprofits can help you when stuck.

Remember, rejection or delays are not your fault.

Nonprofit and Community Support

- **Feeding America (feedingamerica.org):** Food resources.

- **Catholic Charities (catholiccharitiesusa.org):** Emergency aid.

- **National Low Income Housing Coalition (nlihc.org):** Housing resources.

- **AARP (aarp.org):** Help for seniors.

- **Community Action Agencies (communityactionpartnership.com):** Help with LIHEAP, food, or rent.

- **VA Community Resource and Referral Centers (va.gov/homeless/crrc.asp):** Help for veterans.

Some nonprofits require referrals — ask **211** or your local church.

Final Word

The system is built to confuse you. But every locked door has a key if you know who controls it.

Federal funds. State rules. Local chaos.

Start today by calling **211** or visiting **Benefits.gov** to find the right office. Once you learn how to follow the money and track the gatekeepers, you can stop begging and start making tactical moves.

Chapter 5: Filing First, Crying Later

Bureaucracy Doesn't Care If You're Overwhelmed

You can be sick, broke, grieving, or in a full-blown mental health crisis and the system will still tell you that you missed the deadline by one day.

This chapter explains why you should file now, what happens if you miss deadlines, how to appeal, and key phrases to unlock the system.

What Happens When You Miss a Deadline (and What Doesn't)

Missing a deadline does not always kill your chances. It often just moves you to the back of the line or forces you to submit new paperwork. The exact outcome depends on the program.

- **SNAP, Medicaid, and Benefits Applications:**

    - If you miss the due date, you can usually reapply.

    - Some states may backdate benefits if you prove you tried to apply, like with a screenshot, receipt, or denial letter.

    - Backdating varies by state and may require documented proof of your attempt.

- **Social Security (SSI/SSDI):**

    - You have **60 days** to appeal a denial.

    - If you miss this deadline, you can request a late appeal if you show "good cause."

- Reasons like hospitalization, homelessness, mental health crises, or not receiving notice from SSA often qualify.

- Submit hospital records, eviction notices, or other documents with **Form SSA-795** to explain.

- **Housing and Eviction Hearings:**

  - Missing court usually means a default judgment.

  - You may be able to file a motion to vacate or request a new hearing, but deadlines are short, often **7 to 30 days**, depending on your state.

  - Check with the court clerk or use **www.lsc.gov/find-legal-aid** for help.

- **Unemployment Appeals:**

  - These deadlines are strict — often **14 to 30 days** depending on your state.

  - Late submissions need strong evidence, like medical records or employer misconduct documentation.

Late is better than never. File, submit, and ask. You can fix mistakes later.

Winning Appeals with Plain English and Persistence

Most people think they need a lawyer or a perfect legal argument to file an appeal.

They do not.

Appeals are stronger when they:

- Are submitted on time or explain why they are late.

- Clearly explain why the decision was wrong.

- Include new or overlooked information, like updated medical records or written statements.

You do not need legal jargon. You need to be specific, calm, and documented. Persistence counts more than perfect language.

Hearing requests often require a specific form.

- For **SSI/SSDI**, use **SSA-561** for initial appeals and **SSA-3441** for hearing requests. Find both at **SSA.gov**.

- For **SNAP** or **Medicaid**, check your state's DHS website or call **211** for the correct appeal forms.

SSI/SSDI hearings may take **12 to 24 months**. SNAP and Medicaid hearings are usually faster — often **30 to 90 days**.

Hearings may be in-person, virtual, or by phone.

The "Magic Words" That Unlock Bureaucracies

Certain phrases make systems move. Use them clearly and calmly.

- "I would like to request that in writing." This gives you a record.

- "Who supervises this process?" This shows you are serious about following up.

- "Can you show me where that rule is written down?" This makes them prove their decision.

- "I need reasonable accommodation for a disability." This

can include extended deadlines, simpler forms, in-person help, or interpreter services for non-English speakers. Agencies may ask for a doctor's note, but they must respond.

- "I am appealing this decision and requesting a hearing." This protects your rights.

Send requests via email, certified mail, or fax. Save confirmation numbers.

Final Word

You do not have to be emotionally ready to file.

You just have to file.

The system will never warn you when it is your last chance. It will quietly close the door.

Your job is to wedge your foot in that door and say, "Not yet."

File first. Cry later.

You can rest, rage, or grieve once your name is in the system.

Extra Help and Resources

- **SSA.gov:** For SSI/SSDI appeal forms.

- **Benefits.gov** and **211.org:** For program-specific forms, deadlines, and local resources.

- **www.lsc.gov/find-legal-aid:** For free legal help with appeals.

- **HUD.gov/local:** For housing appeal support.

- **CommunityActionPartnership.com:** For emergency food, utility, or rent help.

- **Feeding America (feedingamerica.org):** Emergency food resources.

- **Catholic Charities (catholiccharitiesusa.org):** Emergency aid with multilingual staff.

- **USA.gov:** For federal and state program overviews.

Technology Tips

- Use **Adobe Scan** or similar apps to digitize forms.

- Save confirmation emails or screenshots in a labeled folder.

- Log out of public computers.

- Check denial letters for online appeal options.

- If no portal exists, ask **211** or the agency for paper forms.

Cultural and Language Barriers

- Call **211** for interpreters or help locating translated forms.

- SSA and state DHS sites often have documents in languages like Spanish or Mandarin.

- Libraries, community centers, or nonprofits like **Catholic Charities** may offer translation help.

Mental Health and Motivation

Filing during a crisis can feel impossible. Start with one step. Submit one form. Make one call.

If you are overwhelmed, ask a trusted friend, community center, or church to help.

Rejection or delays are not your fault.

Scams Warning

Scammers may promise faster approvals for a fee.

- Use only official sites like **SSA.gov**, **Benefits.gov**, **HUD.gov**, or state portals.
- Verify suspicious calls with SSA (**1-800-772-1213**) or USDA SNAP (**1-800-221-5689**).

Important Notes on Deadlines and Appeals

- SNAP and Medicaid appeal deadlines vary by state — usually **30 to 90 days**.
- Housing court deadlines are often **7 to 30 days**.
- Unemployment appeals generally have **14 to 30 day** deadlines.
- Agencies may require a doctor's note for reasonable accommodation requests.
- Appeals for **SSI/SSDI** use **Form SSA-561** for reconsideration and **Form SSA-3441** for hearings. Find both at **SSA.gov**.

Nonprofits like **Feeding America**, **Catholic Charities**, or **Community Action Agencies** can provide emergency help during appeal delays.

Chapter 6: How to Read a Government Website Without Losing Your Will to Live

Welcome to the Maze

Government websites are like a game show for the desperate.

- Pick the right form, you win food.

- Pick the wrong form, you get nothing.

- Make a typo, you get kicked back to the start.

They are often outdated, broken on mobile devices, and written in passive-voice legalese designed to make you doubt your intelligence. That is not incompetence, it is insulation. Every extra click shields the agency from dealing with real people.

This chapter shows you how to cut through that nonsense. You will learn how to find what you need, where the real documents live, and how to decode a website built like it is still 2004.

Filters, Maps, and Hidden PDFs

Government sites almost never put what you need on the front page. You will usually find a public relations blurb, a vague mission statement, and a staged photo of people shaking hands.

The real information is usually buried two or three layers deep, often in PDF form, Excel sheets, or inside a half-working "interactive portal."

Look for keywords:

- "Forms and Applications"

- "Eligibility"

- "Document Upload"

- "FAQs" — which are often more helpful than the main instructions.

Pro Tips:

- Agency search bars often miss key documents. Use Google with **site:.gov** plus your keywords.

  - Example: **site:alabama.gov SNAP application PDF**

- Some sites have interactive maps that route you to the right county office. Use them but always double-check the contact info.

- PDFs often contain the actual rules. If you see a page called "Program Guidelines," open it — even if it is long. That is where they hide information you can use to defend yourself.

- Mobile compatibility varies by agency. If a site crashes or loads poorly on your phone, try a desktop or library computer. Some phone browsers allow you to check a setting to go to "desktop mode" which simulates a desktop computer.

- If PDFs are not accessible, you can request an alternative format, like a Word document, under the Americans with Disabilities Act.

- If a site glitches, try clearing your cookies or using your browser's incognito mode.

Agencies That Don't Want You to Know They Exist

Some programs are not even listed on the main agency website. You have to know they exist and go find them.

Examples:

- **Low Income Home Energy Assistance Program (LIHEAP):** Helps with utility bills or energy costs. Often managed by Community Action Agencies or your state's DHS.

- **WIC (Women, Infants, and Children):** Provides food and health support for pregnant women, new mothers, and children under five. Usually handled by state health departments.

- **Medicaid Waivers:** These vary by state and often fall under "Medicaid Services" or "Long-Term Care." They can help people get in-home care instead of being forced into institutions. Call **211** if you cannot find them online.

- **Civil Rights or Fair Housing Offices:** Handle discrimination complaints under the Fair Housing Act. These can be HUD-affiliated or local. Look them up at **hud.gov/program_offices/fair_housing_equal_opp**.

When in doubt: Search Google or Bing with **[your state] [benefit] site:.gov** — this works better than clicking through a homepage.

FOIA, FERPA, and the Records You Can Demand

Sometimes the thing you need is not a benefit, it is information.

There are laws that give you access to documents agencies will not give unless you ask the right way.

- **FOIA (Freedom of Information Act):**
    - Lets you request records from federal agencies like SSA or HUD.
    - Most states have a similar public records law, often called a Freedom of Information Law or Open Records Act.
    - FOIA can be used to request:
        - Case files
        - Email communication between agencies
        - Internal policy memos
    - Agencies may charge fees for large requests or redact sensitive information. Keep your request narrow and specific to avoid delays.
    - Example: You were denied help and want to know why. You can FOIA your case notes.
- **FERPA (Family Educational Rights and Privacy Act):**
    - Lets students or parents of minors request school records such as grades, discipline files, special education records.
    - Applies to K–12 schools and higher education.
    - Schools must allow inspection and review of records within **45 days**. They may charge for copies but must allow free inspection.

How to Use These Tools:

- Always make your request in writing.
- Use clear language like:
    - "This is a request under the Freedom of Information Act (FOIA)."
    - Or: "This is a request under the [Your State] Open Records Act."
- Be specific. Include dates, names, and exactly what you want.

Agencies are required by law to respond. They may delay, deny, or redact but if you push, the law is on your side.

Final Word

Government websites are not broken. They are working exactly as designed — to slow you down and frustrate you into giving up.

If you learn how to read past the slogans, dig into the PDFs, and use search engines like scalpels, you can pull real power out of them.

You do not need a degree to navigate these sites. You need grit, a few keywords, and a refusal to let bad design shut you out.

If you made it this far, you are already ahead of the people trying to keep you in the dark.

Chapter 7: What You Can Say to a Cop and Still Go Home

You're Not Powerless. But You're Not Safe, Either.

There is a myth in America that if you are innocent, respectful, and compliant, nothing bad will happen during a police encounter.

There is another myth that you can "know your rights" and always walk away untouched.

Both are lies. The truth lives in the tension. You have rights but only if you know how to use them without escalating risk.

Your rights include:

- **Fourth Amendment:** Protection against unreasonable searches and seizures.

- **Fifth Amendment:** The right to remain silent.

- **Sixth Amendment:** The right to a lawyer.

Risks vary depending on location, the discretion of the officer, and systemic biases. These risks are often higher for marginalized groups. Staying calm matters.

This chapter is a reality-based guide for dealing with police in real life, not in theory. It will not protect you in every situation, but it will help you survive the ones that can still be won.

Your Only Real Goals

When you are stopped by police, you have exactly three goals:

1. Stay alive.

2. Avoid arrest.

3. Preserve your rights if number two fails.

You are not trying to win an argument.

You are not trying to educate them.

You are not trying to show them up.

The side of the road is not the courtroom.

You can file a complaint later. You can sue later. But first, you have to survive the stop.

The Golden Phrases

These are the baseline phrases you should memorize. You do not need to say them all at once. You need to say the right one at the right moment.

- **"Am I being detained, or am I free to go?"**
    - If they say you are free to go, leave.
    - If they say you are being detained, stop talking.
    - Police must have reasonable suspicion to detain you or probable cause to arrest you. If they lack it, your lawyer can challenge the stop later.
- **"I do not consent to any searches."**
    - Say this calmly, clearly, and on record.
    - Even if they search you anyway, your refusal matters in court.
    - Never say, "I do not have anything" or "Go ahead."

43

That is giving consent.

- **"I'm going to remain silent. I would like a lawyer."**

  - This activates your right to remain silent and your right to an attorney.

  - Say it clearly and **stop talking**.

  - This stops questioning if you are in custody. During a stop, police may continue casual conversation.

- **"I want to speak to my lawyer before answering any questions."**

  - Use this if you are already in custody or at the station.

  - They are required to stop questioning you.

Some states offer extra protections. For example, California's Right to Know Act requires officers to explain detainment if asked. Check your state laws at **www.aclu.org**.

What NOT to Do

- Do not argue or raise your voice.

- Do not run.

- Do not lie.

- Do not consent to searches.

- Do not try to film secretly. If recording is legal in your state, film openly.

Do not say:

- "I know my rights." It sounds combative and may escalate things.

- "You can't do this." They can. They are. Let your lawyer say that later.

Lying can lead to charges like obstruction of justice. Silence is safer.

In states with two-party consent laws like California or Florida, do not secretly record audio in private spaces.

When You're a Passenger

If you are in a car that gets pulled over:

- You do not have to answer questions.

- You do not have to consent to a search.

- You can ask if you are free to leave.

- If they say yes, leave quietly.

- If they say no, **stop talking**.

In some states, passengers must show ID if police have reasonable suspicion. Check your state's stop-and-identify laws.

When Things Go Bad Anyway

Sometimes you say all the right things, and they arrest you anyway.

If that happens:

- You said, "I'm remaining silent," and followed through.

- You said, "I do not consent."
- You did not fight, lie, or flee.

This helps your defense later. Judges and juries are more likely to side with someone who stayed calm and clear.

If arrested, contact **Legal Aid (www.lsc.gov/find-legal-aid)** or request a public defender. They can challenge unlawful stops or searches.

Recording the Police

In most states, you have the right to film police in public if you do not interfere.

- Do not record in restricted areas.
- Do not hide your camera in a two-party consent state.

Some states, like Arizona, restrict filming within a certain distance (for example, within eight feet).

Best Practices:

- Start recording as soon as contact begins.
- State your name and location out loud.
- Use apps like **ACLU Mobile Justice** or **Bambuser** to auto-upload video to the cloud.
- Save emergency contacts in your phone.

Final Word

You do not have to be fearless.

You do not have to be a lawyer.

You have to stay calm, speak clearly, and know when to stop talking.

Most people incriminate themselves because they think they have to explain. You do not.

You have the right to remain silent but **you have to use it**.

In a broken system, survival means learning the script.

So learn it.

Extra Help and Resources

- **www.aclu.org/know-your-rights** — State-specific guides.
- **www.lsc.gov/find-legal-aid** — Legal Aid services.
- **nlg.org** — National Lawyers Guild for protest support and rights violations.
- **NAACP.org** and local community organizations — Community support and training.
- **ACLU Mobile Justice** or **Bambuser** — Apps for recording and auto-upload.

If English is not your first language:

- Say, "I need an interpreter."
- Use translated rights cards from **ACLU.org**.
- Contact Legal Aid or community centers for post-arrest support.

Police encounters can be terrifying, especially for marginalized groups. Practice these phrases in advance. Community groups can offer training or support.

Beware of scams offering fake legal services. Use free resources like **www.aclu.org** or **www.lsc.gov/find-legal-aid**.

Police body camera footage can often be requested later through a FOIA request.

Community organizations often provide training on handling police encounters.

Chapter 8: Eviction and Housing Triage

When the Sheriff Shows Up, It's Already Too Late

Most people do not understand eviction law until they are already locked out of their home. By then, the system has moved on.

This chapter is about acting fast, knowing your rights, and learning how to buy time legally. You may not win forever, but you can stall, negotiate, or reposition. Sometimes, that is all you need.

The First Rule: Don't Wait for the Court Date

The second you get a notice — whether it's taped to your door, slid under it, or mailed to you — act immediately.

Eviction notices fall into two categories:

- **"Pay or Quit"** — You owe rent. Pay now or move out. This notice often gives you three to seven days to pay or leave, depending on your state.

- **"Notice to Terminate Tenancy"** — They want you gone for other reasons. These notices may give you thirty to sixty days, depending on state law.

These are not court orders. They are warnings. If you respond now, you may be able to:

- Pay back rent and stay.

- Work out a payment plan.

- Buy time before a formal eviction is filed.

Notices must be served legally — usually by posting, mailing, or hand-delivery. Improper service, like email in some states, may make a notice invalid. Check your state's rules.

Every day matters. The longer you wait, the fewer options you will have.

Know Your State's Laws — They Decide Everything

Eviction laws are local. What is legal in one state may be illegal in another.

Key differences by state include:

- How much notice your landlord must give.
- Whether they can evict you without cause.
- Whether you get a hearing before the lockout.
- Whether you have a grace period to fix the problem.

Some states, like Oregon, ban no-cause evictions for long-term tenants. Others, like Texas or Florida, allow them with proper notice.

Find your state's tenant guide or legal aid eviction FAQ by searching:

[Your State] tenant rights eviction site:.gov

Or check **www.lsc.gov/find-legal-aid** and your state's housing department website.

Legal Triage: Your Tools and Tactics

Ways to buy time or stop an eviction:

1. **Answer the Lawsuit**

   - If they file formal eviction papers, respond within the deadline — often five to fourteen days.

   - Even a simple statement like, "I disagree with the claim and request a hearing," delays judgment and secures a court date.

2. **Ask for a Continuance**

   - If you are not ready for court, ask the judge for more time.

   - Judges may grant a short continuance if you need legal help or documents. These are not guaranteed.

3. **Challenge Bad Paperwork**

   - If the notice was missing information, filed too early, or served improperly, it may be invalid. Judges do not always catch mistakes, but you can bring them up.

4. **Claim Retaliation or Discrimination**

   - If you recently complained about repairs, used a housing voucher, or belong to a protected class (race, disability, family status, etc.), you may have a defense.

   - Contact a Fair Housing Office for help with these claims.

5. **Offer to Pay and Stay**

   - In many states, paying what you owe cancels the eviction. This is called "curing the default."

- It usually only works before a final judgment.

Code Violations as Leverage

If your rental is unsafe (mold, pests, broken heat) you may be able to:

- Delay eviction by requesting inspections.
- Force repairs before they can evict you.
- Trigger a city investigation that buys time.

Use smart tactics:

- File complaints in writing or online with your local health or building department.
- Take photos and keep copies.
- Never stop paying rent unless your state's law allows it.

Some states allow "repair and deduct" or rent escrow for major violations. Check with Legal Aid first.

Emergency Aid: Who Has the Money

Emergency funds may be available, but finding them can take work.

Check with:

- County Human Services or Housing Authority.
- **211.org** for local nonprofit support.
- Catholic Charities, Salvation Army, or Legal Aid.
- Tenant unions or mutual aid groups.

- **LIHEAP (communityactionpartnership.com)** for utility-related eviction support.

- **National Low Income Housing Coalition (nlihc.org)** for local rental assistance programs.

Some landlords will pause an eviction if you apply for aid, even if you have not been approved yet.

After the Lockout: What Next?

If you are locked out:

- Retrieve your belongings quickly. States often require landlords to store them for seven to thirty days, and you may have to pay storage fees.

- Request court records. You may be able to seal or expunge the eviction later, though this is limited and usually requires legal help.

- Do not sign anything you do not understand, especially move-out agreements that waive rights.

Then:

- Apply for emergency housing.

- Look into housing-first nonprofits.

- Consider moving to another county if services there move faster.

Final Word

Eviction is not always beatable, but it is almost always delayable.

Sometimes, a delay is enough to find your footing.

The law will not protect you unless you invoke it — on paper, in court, and in time.

Stand up early. Show up on time. Do not panic.

Most of the power comes from refusing to go quietly.

Extra Resources:

- **<u>www.lsc.gov/find-legal-aid</u>** — Legal Aid for eviction help.

- **nlihc.org** — National Low Income Housing Coalition for rental aid programs.

- **tenantunion.org** — Tenant unions and advocacy groups.

- **hud.gov/program_offices/fair_housing_equal_opp** — Fair Housing Office for discrimination claims.

- **211.org** — Emergency assistance contacts.

- **communityactionpartnership.com** — Find LIHEAP and local community aid.

Federal programs like the Emergency Rental Assistance Program may still be available in some areas. Check **nlihc.org** for updates.

Chapter 9: Debt — What They Can (and Can't) Do to You

You Don't Owe Fear

Most debt is not a moral failure. It is math. You did not get crushed because you bought too much coffee. You got crushed because rent is twelve hundred dollars and your check is nine hundred fifty.

Still, the way debt collectors talk to you would make you think you committed a felony. But debt is not jail time. And most of what they threaten you with they cannot actually do.

This chapter is your shield: what debt collectors are allowed to do, what they are bluffing about, and how to stop the bleeding without wrecking your life.

Let's Get One Thing Straight: You Can't Go to Jail for Owing Money to a Creditor

This is the first and most important rule.

You cannot be jailed for not paying:

- Credit cards.
- Medical bills.
- Payday loans.
- Rent (unless you violate a court order).
- Utility bills.

If someone tells you otherwise, they are lying.

But you *can* be jailed for certain debts tied to court orders, like child support or court fines. That is because missing those payments can lead to contempt of court charges which is a legal violation, not a debt issue.

You can be sued. You can get a judgment. But jail? Not for debt. The United States banned debtors' prisons over a century ago.

However, ignoring a court order — like failing to appear for a court hearing — could lead to contempt of court, which carries a risk of jail. Also, debts involving fraud, like lying to obtain a loan, could lead to separate criminal charges.

What Creditors Can Actually Do

There are only three real enforcement tools and they all require going through court.

1. **Lawsuit**

   - They sue you in civil court. If you do not respond, they win by default.

   - If you do respond, they have to prove you owe it.

2. **Judgment**

   - If they win the lawsuit, they get a judgment.

   - This lets them pursue collection methods like garnishment or liens.

3. **Enforcement**

   - Depending on your state, they may:

     - Garnish your wages — usually capped at

twenty-five percent of disposable income under federal law, with some states having stricter limits.

- Put a lien on property.

- Freeze a bank account — though many states protect a basic amount, often between one thousand and five thousand dollars, for living expenses.

Certain income sources — like Social Security, SSI, and some pensions — are usually exempt from garnishment. Check your state laws.

What They Can't Do Without a Judge

Collectors cannot:

- Take your paycheck directly.

- Freeze your account on demand.

- Take your house, car, or anything else.

- Call your job and "notify your employer." They can verify employment but not disclose your debt.

- Threaten arrest.

The Fair Debt Collection Practices Act (FDCPA) applies to third-party collectors — not original creditors like banks — and forbids these tactics.

When You Can Ignore Them

You do not have to answer every call or letter. You have the legal right to tell them to stop contacting you.

Send a written letter that says:

"Under the Fair Debt Collection Practices Act, I am requesting that you cease all communication regarding this debt."

Send it via certified mail or email with receipt confirmation for proof.

This does not erase the debt, but it stops harassment.

You should respond if:

- You are being sued.
- You receive something from a court and not just a debt collector.
- You are within the statute of limitations and might settle.

If it is old, expired debt or harassment, you do not owe them your time.

Statute of Limitations: When Debt Expires

Each state sets a time limit on how long a debt can be collected through the courts. This is called the statute of limitations.

It ranges from three to ten years depending on:

- The type of debt — credit, medical, auto.
- The state where you lived when you took it on.

After that time runs out, they cannot sue you.

However, making a payment, admitting the debt in writing, or even promising to pay can restart the clock in some states.

Always check your state statutes via reliable sites like **nolo.com** or state consumer protection websites.

Bankruptcy: The Nuclear Option (That Works)

If your debts are unpayable and lawsuits are stacking up, bankruptcy may be the smart move.

There are two types:

- **Chapter 7:** Wipes most debts clean, fast.

- **Chapter 13:** Sets up a payment plan based on what you can afford.

Bankruptcy will not erase:

- Child support.

- Some taxes.

- Federal student loans — unless you prove undue hardship, which is rare but possible.

But it will stop:

- Lawsuits.

- Garnishments.

- Harassment.

- Collection calls.

Filing fees are around three hundred to four hundred dollars, though fee waivers may be available for low-income filers.

Bankruptcy is not failure. It is a legal tool built for exactly this situation when the numbers no longer add up.

Credit Scores Are Rebuildable

You may lose points. You may lose your score entirely.

So what?

- Scores can be rebuilt.

- Lenders reset risk every few years.

- You can live, rent, and work without a perfect number.

- You can often get a secured credit card within months of bankruptcy.

- Negative marks like bankruptcy fall off your credit report after seven to ten years.

You are not your credit score. You are not your balance sheet. Anyone who says otherwise is either selling something or collecting something.

Final Word

Debt collectors rely on fear.

They want you to believe the phone call is the law, the letter is the judgment, and that you are the criminal.

You are not.

Debt is a civil issue. You owe money. That is it. You do not owe your dignity, your peace, or your silence.

If you fight smart, document everything, and know your limits, you win back control.

Even if you are broke.

Extra Resources:

- **www.consumerfinance.gov** — For FDCPA complaints and debt guides.
- **www.lsc.gov/find-legal-aid** — Free bankruptcy or lawsuit help.
- **www.nolo.com** — State-specific statute of limitations charts.
- **naag.org** — State attorney general contacts for consumer protection.
- **nfcc.org** — National Foundation for Credit Counseling for free debt management plans.

Scams Warning:

Beware of fake collectors demanding immediate payment.

- Always verify debts with original creditors or by checking **consumerfinance.gov**.

Debt Validation:

You can request debt validation within thirty days of first contact under the FDCPA. This forces collectors to prove the debt is real.

Chapter 10: What Happens If You Just… Don't Show Up to Court?

Spoiler: The World Doesn't End But It Might Get Way Harder

Sometimes you are too sick. Sometimes you are frozen in panic. Sometimes the court date comes and goes and you just… do not show up.

If that is you, this chapter is not here to scold you. It is here to tell you what happens next and how to fix it if you are ready.

The Truth About Missing Court

When you miss a court date, the judge does not assume you are innocent or busy. They generally assume you do not care and they usually just rule against you.

Here is what that looks like depending on the case:

- **Eviction Hearing:**
    - You are ruled against by default.
    - You may get locked out within three to ten days, depending on your state's laws.
    - In some states, you can file a motion to vacate and ask for a new hearing.

- **Debt Lawsuit:**
    - You get a default judgment.
    - That judgment can lead to garnishments, bank

freezes, or property liens.

- Debt judgments can last seven to twenty years and may be renewed in some states.

- You can challenge the judgment later but it is harder.

- **Criminal Case or Traffic Violation:**

  - A bench warrant may be issued.

  - Bench warrants for traffic violations will not trigger manhunts but can lead to arrest during routine stops.

  - Some judges will cancel the warrant if you appear voluntarily.

Bench Warrants: What They Are and Aren't

A bench warrant is not the same as a criminal arrest warrant. It is a judicial order that says:

"This person failed to appear. Detain them and bring them to court."

Police are not out hunting you. But they will run your name if you:

- Get pulled over.

- Apply for a government job.

- Try to renew a license or ID in some states.

Bench warrants are logged in databases like NCIC (National Crime Information Center) and may affect background checks, licenses, or jobs.

You can fix it. In many cases, you can:

- Call the clerk's office.
- Ask if the warrant can be recalled.
- You may need to file a motion to quash the warrant, which could involve a fee or hearing.
- Schedule a new court date and show up.

Judges often prefer a voluntary appearance over wasting time and jail space. Do not wait for cuffs.

What Judges Will Forgive (If You Ask the Right Way)

Judges are human. They will not forgive everything, but they often reconsider if you:

- Show up voluntarily.
- Bring documentation — illness, homelessness, mental health issues, etc.
- Are respectful and honest.

Show "good cause," like hospital records or eviction notices, to explain your absence.

Key phrase:

"Your honor, I did not understand what I was supposed to do. I am here now because I want to fix it."

That alone can reopen doors. In many civil cases, they will vacate the default and let you defend yourself.

What Happens If You Ignore It Forever

Some things do fade. Most do not.

- **Debts:**
  - Statutes of limitation are typically three to seven years.
  - Creditors may move on.
  - Judgments last years and can renew.
- **Evictions:**
  - Stay on your tenant screening reports for seven years.
  - Make it harder to rent again.
  - Some can be sealed with legal help.
- **Warrants:**
  - Do not expire.
  - Are typically state-specific but may appear nationwide for serious cases.
  - Can affect background checks, licenses, and jobs.

If you are thinking long-term — jobs, housing, kids — cleaning this up now is easier than dealing with bigger problems later.

How to Come Back

If you are ready to stop running, here is how to start:

1. **Call the clerk of the court** where the issue happened. Ask

if there is a warrant, default, or judgment.

2. **Ask what can be done.** Use the phrase:

   - **"I would like to resolve this voluntarily. What are my options?"**

3. **Get on the calendar.** Ask to set a hearing or motion date.

4. **Bring documentation.** Medical records, eviction notices, hospital stays — anything that proves why you were in crisis.

5. **Show up.** Calm, clean, and clear. No speeches. No blame. Just intent to fix.

Contact **www.lsc.gov/find-legal-aid** for help filing motions to vacate judgments or quash warrants. Motions may cost twenty to one hundred dollars, but fee waivers are available for low-income individuals. If your issue involves a criminal or traffic warrant, request a public defender.

Tenant screening services, like TransUnion or Experian, report evictions. If there is an error, you can file a dispute.

You do not need to beg. You just need to face it.

Final Word

You are not the first person to miss a deadline.

You are not the first to ghost the system.

And you will not be the last to walk back in and win.

Do not let shame talk you out of action.

Do not let fear tell you it is too late.

Most of the power is still on the table if you are willing to sit down again.

Chapter 11: Hiding in the Open — How to Stay Private in 2025

You Don't Need to Disappear. You Just Need to Get Boring.

Most people think staying private means going off-grid, smashing your phone, and building a bunker. That is fantasy.

In the real world, you do not have to vanish. You just have to stop bleeding data from every hole.

This chapter is not about paranoia. It is about control. Who gets your information, how often, and for what purpose. You are not trying to be invisible. You are trying to stop handing over ammunition to systems that do not serve you.

The Myth of "Nothing to Hide"

They will tell you if you have done nothing wrong, you have nothing to hide.

That is nonsense.

- You are allowed to protect your medical history. HIPAA protects your medical data, but only from certain types of disclosure.

- You are allowed to limit who knows where you sleep.

- You are allowed to keep your name off lists.

- You are allowed to avoid being tracked, profiled, or sold.

Privacy is not guilt. It is defense. Companies exploit vague consent forms or fine print to track you. Read the terms before you agree.

Phones: Your Pocket Snitch

Your phone is the single biggest data leak in your life.

What it shares by default:

- Location.

- App usage.

- Microphone access.

- Search history.

- Contacts and call logs.

- Biometric data — face, fingerprint, and more.

What to do about it:

1. **Location Settings**

   - Turn off location sharing and ad personalization in system settings.

   - On iOS, disable "Precise Location" for apps. On Android, use "Approximate Location."

   - Disable location access for all apps except maps and even then, only "while using."

2. **Stop Using Your Real Number**

   - Use a second number through apps like Google Voice, TextNow, or Burner.

   - Give that number to doctors, landlords, job applications — not your main line.

- Some services, like banks, may not accept VOIP numbers like Google Voice.

3. **Use Airplane Mode When You Can**

- Even with GPS off, phones still ping towers. Going offline is the only reliable silence.

4. **Ditch Biometric Unlocking**

- Courts often allow forced biometric unlocking. Your passcode is protected under the Fifth Amendment but your fingerprint and face are not.

Browsers, Search Engines, and Digital Trails

Most people use Chrome and Google. That is like living in a glass house while shouting your Social Security number.

Switch to:

- Firefox or Brave for browsing.

- DuckDuckGo or Startpage for search.

- uBlock Origin and Privacy Badger to block trackers. These work best on desktop; mobile browsers may need built-in blockers.

- VPNs if you need to mask your location or dodge surveillance — but do not assume they are bulletproof.

Also:

- Clear cookies regularly.

- Avoid auto-logins.

- Do not reuse passwords. Use a password manager like

Bitwarden or LastPass.

When a VPN Is Useless

VPNs are hyped as cure-alls. They are not.

VPNs will not protect you from:

- Logging into Facebook under your real name.

- Using your personal Gmail.

- Filling out forms with your real information.

- Buying things with your debit card.

Use VPNs to:

- Avoid IP tracking.

- Spoof your location.

- Stop your internet service provider from watching your traffic.

Avoid free VPNs — they may log your data. Use paid services like ProtonVPN or PIA.

But remember: if the account is tied to you, it does not matter where the traffic comes from.

Real-World Privacy Tricks That Actually Work

1. **Use a PO Box or Mailbox Service**

   - Stop giving your street address to everyone. USPS PO boxes cost $20–$100 per year. Private mailbox services are pricier but offer flexibility.

2. **Pay in Cash When You Can**

  - Especially for things that signal patterns — gas, groceries, medication.

  - For rentals or bills, get a receipt for proof of payment.

3. **Obfuscate Birthdays and Email Info**

  - You do not have to lie. Leave blanks or use a decoy birthday or email for loyalty programs, free trials, and other non-essentials.

4. **Stop Filling Out Every Form**

  - They ask because most people answer. If it is not required, skip it. "Prefer not to say" is a complete sentence.

5. **Make Yourself Boring to Track**

  - Use default settings.

  - Do not click wild links.

  - Do not give platforms personality data.

  - Keep your online presence fragmented — one account for work, another for social, another for activism.

What the Government (and Corporations) Track

Depending on what you have touched, your profile may include:

- Credit history and rent payment data.

- Cell tower pings.

- Facial recognition from DMV photos or surveillance cameras.

- Purchases and transaction patterns.

- Medicaid or SSI status.

- Social media accounts.

You cannot erase all of it.

But you can:

- Slow the data drip.

- Refuse new leaks.

- Avoid cross-connecting systems.

- Opt out of data brokers — visit **optoutprescreen.com** or **privacyrights.org**.

Final Word

You do not need to hide. You need to choose what gets seen.

Privacy is not about shame. It is about survival. It is about not feeding data into the same machine that has been grinding you down.

They already have too much.

Let that be the last free piece.

Extra Resources:

- **<u>www.eff.org</u>** — Electronic Frontier Foundation for privacy guides and tools.

- **optoutprescreen.com** — Limit credit data sharing.

- www.privacyrights.org — Data broker opt-outs.

- www.nolo.com — Consumer protection laws.

Real-Life Tips:

- Check phone settings weekly for sneaky app permissions.

- Use Signal or WhatsApp for encrypted messaging.

- Save privacy settings screenshots in a "Privacy" folder.

- Beware of fake privacy apps or VPNs that steal data.

Cultural and Language Barriers:

If English is not your first language, use translated privacy guides at **eff.org** or ask libraries for help with phone settings.

Social Media Privacy:

- Limit public posts.

- Disable location tags.

- Separate personal, work, and activism accounts.

Data Broker Opt-Outs:

Consider services like DeleteMe or manually opt out using **privacyrights.org**.

Chapter 12: The AI Tools That Work (And the Ones That Lie)

Somewhere Between Useless and Magic

AI is not going to save the world.

It is also not going to kill you in your sleep.

It is just a tool. Like a microwave. If you know what buttons to press, you get hot food. If not, you blow up a fork.

Most of the hype around AI is distraction in the forms of venture capital, weird headlines, and nonsense futurism. But under all that, there are real tools that can help you survive, save time, and outthink the systems designed to confuse you.

This chapter is about using AI tactically and avoiding the stuff that will steer you straight into a wall.

What AI Can Actually Help With (Right Now)

1. **Bureaucratic Writing**

Use AI tools to:

- Draft appeal letters.
- Write emails to agencies.
- Fill out forms in formal language.
- Explain confusing documents in plain English.

Check AI-generated letters for accuracy and make sure the tone matches what the agency expects. Do not assume the draft is correct without reviewing.

75

Example Prompt:

"Write an appeal letter for a denied SNAP application. I was rejected because they counted my roommate's income, but we do not share food or expenses."

Refine from there. These tools are tireless and they will not judge you.

2. Job Applications

AI can help with:

- Writing resumes from scratch.
- Editing cover letters.
- Tailoring language to job postings.
- Prepping answers for interview questions.

You still need to check it. But if you are too tired to start from zero, this can break the block.

3. Legal and Policy Translation

AI can break down legalese, government contracts, or court paperwork into readable chunks.

Try prompts like:

- "Explain this Social Security denial letter like I am 12."
- "Turn this lease clause into plain English."
- "What does this eviction notice actually mean?"

AI can explain the basics but may miss critical state-specific details. Verify anything important with www.lsc.gov/find-legal-aid or your state court website.

4. **Medical Decoding**

You can paste a discharge summary or diagnosis and ask:

- "What does this mean in regular language?"
- "What questions should I ask my doctor about this?"
- "Is this urgent?"

Do not use AI to self-diagnose. Use it to understand terms before talking to a doctor.

AI That Lies, Hallucinates, or Gets You Killed

AI is not perfect. It does not know things. It predicts likely answers based on patterns.

That means:

- It can make up laws that sound real.
- It can confidently explain fake programs.
- It can give outdated information that sounds current.

AI may hallucinate plausible-sounding answers that are completely wrong. Always verify with .gov sites, official forms, or legal aid.

Never trust AI for:

- Court deadlines.
- Exact legal advice.
- State-specific benefit rules.
- Real-time emergency information.

Use it to generate starting points, summaries, or drafts. Then verify **everything** before acting on it.

Free and Low-Cost AI Tools Worth Using

- **ChatGPT (Free or Plus):**
    - Text-based. Excellent for writing, summarizing, and explaining.
    - Free tier is limited; paid Plus ($20/month) offers better access.

- **Perplexity.ai:**
    - Better for current events and fact-checked answers. Links sources. Great for looking things up safely.
    - Free tier is robust; paid upgrades (~$20/month) for heavy use.

- **Claude (Anthropic):**
    - Similar to ChatGPT but often more concise. Offers free access with optional paid upgrades.

- **Google Gemini:**
    - Built into Android and Google products. Fast, but often inaccurate. Always double-check.

- **Grok 3:**
    - Available on grok.com, x.com, and mobile apps. Free basic use with optional SuperGrok subscription for higher limits. Strong for drafting letters and explaining documents.

How to Prompt Like a Pro

AI is not human. It does not know what you meant unless you spell it out.

Tips:

- Be specific: "Write like I am applying for food stamps, not a college scholarship."

- Give context: "This is for someone with PTSD and limited income."

- Break it down: Ask one task at a time, not ten at once.

- Refine the response if it is off. Follow up with more details or corrections.

Bad Prompt:

"Write a good letter."

Good Prompt:

"Write a polite but firm letter asking for Medicaid reinstatement after being cut off for missing a deadline."

The more you feed in, the better the output.

AI Tools That Are Probably Useless for You (For Now)

- AI image generators — unless you are an artist or meme-maker.

- AI trading bots — you will lose money.

- AI life coaches — glorified journaling apps.

- AI mental health chatbots — often privacy risks and

dangerously unqualified.

- Voice clones or deepfakes — cool, but legally risky.

If you do not need it, skip it. Most of this tech is shiny distraction. You are trying to survive and adapt — not help build Skynet.

Final Word

You do not have to worship AI.

You do not have to fear it.

You just have to use it better than the people who want you confused.

It is a lever. Not a miracle. Not a threat. Just a machine that helps you push back if you learn how to pull the handle.

Use it smart. Check its work. Keep your power.

Chapter 13: How to Build a Paper Trail That Protects You

You're Not Paranoid. You're Just Unarmed Without Proof.

In every system that decides whether you eat, get housed, or stay out of jail, documentation is king.

You can cry, explain, plead, or scream. None of it will matter if you cannot show a receipt, a copy, or a timestamp. Bureaucracy does not believe people. It believes paper.

This chapter shows how to build that paper trail, not for courtrooms or speeches, but for basic survival. If you are broke, sick, or under pressure, this is your armor.

Why Documentation Wins

Because the people deciding your case:

- Do not know you.

- Do not care about your story.

- Want to close the file without getting sued.

When they see you have documented everything — dates, names, calls, letters — they get cautious. You become a risk to mishandle. That is power.

Documentation can also strengthen appeals or lawsuits under laws like the Administrative Procedure Act. Keep your records for at least three to seven years, as agencies may request them for audits, appeals, or disputes.

Start with the Basics: What to Track and Keep

Conversations with Any Agency:

- Write down the date, time, and full name of the person you spoke to.

- Note what they said and what you were told to do.

- Keep this in a notebook or phone file labeled by topic (SNAP, SSI, housing).

- In one-party consent states, you can legally record the call, but check your state's laws at www.nolo.com.

Applications and Forms:

- Screenshot or print every page before hitting submit.

- Save confirmation numbers.

- If mailed, use certified mail or keep a picture of the envelope and form.

- Include your application or case number in every letter.

Denial Letters:

- Keep the original and scan a copy.

- Highlight the reason for denial. It shapes your appeal.

- Under federal law, agencies must provide written denial reasons. Request one if they do not.

Medical or Legal Documents:

- Always ask for a copy of your own file.

- Organize chronologically, oldest to newest.

- Do not assume anyone else will share your records with another agency. You are the bridge.

Letters, Not Phone Calls

If it matters, write it down and send it.

Phone calls disappear. Letters do not.

Use clear, formal language. Keep it short. Date everything.

Example format:

Jane Smith
123 N Example St
Anytown, ST 12345
July 5, 2025

To Whom It May Concern,

I am writing to request a copy of the denial explanation for my Medicaid application submitted on June 15, 2025. I believe there may have been an error.

Please respond in writing. Thank you.

Sincerely,
Jane Smith

Always keep a copy. If mailed, keep proof. If emailed, BCC yourself or use a secure email service like ProtonMail.

Keep a Timeline File

One of the strongest tools you can hand a lawyer, judge, or caseworker is a simple timeline.

Create a file (Word document, Google document, or notebook) that lists:

- Dates.

- Events (submitted forms, received letters, phone calls, denials).

- Outcomes.

Example:

- 5/2/25: Applied for SNAP online.

- 5/10/25: Called office — told "pending."

- 5/20/25: Denial letter received — stated "missing income verification."

- 5/21/25: Faxed missing documents.

- 6/2/25: No response — called again.

This turns chaos into clarity. It shows you are not confused — they are. Share your timeline with Legal Aid to strengthen your appeal or lawsuit.

Record What They Don't Expect You To

Agencies do not expect you to:

- Record in-person conversations in a notebook.

- Ask for receipts for everything.

- Follow up with a "per our conversation" email.

They assume you will forget, misstate, or vanish. That assumption helps them close your file.

Break that assumption. Be the person who follows up, tracks names, and saves every scrap. You do not need to be perfect, just harder to dismiss than the average applicant.

Organizing Without Burning Out

You do not need a fancy system. Just:

- A folder on your phone or computer for each issue (SNAP, rent, disability).

- A simple naming system, like medicaid_denial_07-05-25.pdf.

- A spiral notebook or Google Doc to log all conversations.

- A backup method, such as emailing files to yourself or storing them in the cloud.

- Use free cloud storage services like Google Drive or Dropbox.

If you can only do one thing, take a photo of every letter you get and put it in a folder labeled "Govt Docs."

That alone beats ninety percent of what they expect.

When to Bring the Paper

Times to bring your documentation:

- Court hearings.

- Appeals.

- Meetings with social workers, case managers, or nonprofit aid organizations.

- Emergency rooms or clinics.

- Reapplication interviews.

- Audits or disputes with agencies.

You do not need to be combative. You do need to be prepared. When you pull out a binder or phone folder, the tone of the room changes.

Final Word

You are not building a paper trail because you love bureaucracy.

You are building it because you have been lied to, forgotten, or blamed before.

Your records are proof you were there. That you asked. That you complied. That you did not just disappear.

Paper cannot protect you from everything. But in a system that runs on denials and delays, it is the closest thing to a shield you have.

Use it.

Extras That Might Help:

- Keep tax records for seven years.

- Keep benefits records for at least three years.

- Some agencies accept digital signatures via tools like DocuSign.

- Use FOIA to request agency records at usa.gov/foia.

Chapter 14: Mutual Aid Without Getting Raided

The Government Has a Funny Definition of "Helping People"

If you feed people regularly without a permit, you might get shut down. If you offer housing during a freeze without proper zoning, you could get fined. If you distribute free medication or harm reduction supplies, you may be accused of endangerment or "practicing medicine without a license."

Mutual aid scares power. It exposes the failure of the system by showing that people are willing to care for each other without profit or authority. This chapter will not tell you to stop helping. It will tell you how to do it in a way that keeps you and your community safer.

Mutual Aid Is Not Charity

Charity is what wealthy people do to feel good. It usually comes with strings, branding, surveillance, or forced gratitude.

Mutual aid is different. It is horizontal. Someone gives what they can, and someone receives what they need. It might look like free groceries, a cash app fund for someone's electric bill, or a rotation of safe crash spots for unhoused neighbors.

Once mutual aid becomes visible, local governments often respond with suspicion. They assume it must be fraud, trespassing, or a threat to order. Sometimes they are right. Usually they are just uncomfortable watching people do their job better than they do.

Mutual aid operates in a legal gray zone because it often lacks formal structure, making it subject to local ordinances. Groups like Food Not Bombs and Mutual Aid Disaster Relief often provide examples of both effective community help and legal challenges.

The Line Between Legal and "Disruptive"

Most mutual aid work exists in this legally gray area. You are unlikely to be prosecuted for handing out sandwiches in a park, but you might get shut down, ticketed, or harassed if it becomes regular or politically visible.

Common triggers for backlash:

- Repeated gatherings without permits.

- Distributions that attract large crowds or media attention.

- Activities involving tents, generators, propane, or long-term presence.

- Unlicensed distribution of medication, especially controlled substances.

- Aid that becomes a political statement.

Cities may require permits for public food distribution or gatherings over fifty people. Check your local ordinances. Sharing prescription drugs is illegal under federal law. Stick to items like Narcan or over-the-counter supplies when helping with harm reduction.

If you stay under the radar, most jurisdictions will ignore you. Once you get press or pushback from local officials, expect zoning laws, health codes, and noise ordinances to be used against you.

What You Can Do Openly

You can almost always:

- Give people cash or gift cards.

- Cook food in your home and deliver it to friends.

- Let someone stay in your private residence.

- Post bail for someone, though some states monitor bail funds.

- Provide transportation.

- Share clothing, supplies, or tools.

- Help someone fill out forms or navigate systems.

None of that requires permission. Unless you are doing it at scale or in public, it is almost impossible to stop.

How to Distribute Food and Supplies Safely

If you are organizing food distribution, be aware of local food safety laws. Some cities require permits for public feeding, even if it is free. Others ignore small operations.

To reduce risk:

- Distribute on private property with the owner's consent.

- Avoid setting up permanent stations without a permit.

- Use individually packaged items when possible.

- Keep the group small and quiet.

- Know your neighbors and build trust before making it public.

Cities like Houston and Los Angeles have strict public feeding bans. Check local laws at city websites or municode.com. Many groups solve this with a text chain or mutual aid group chat. Someone says, "I have twenty boxes of produce," and others quietly arrange pickup. No permits. No exposure.

Money: How to Move It Without Trouble

Moving money through mutual aid can attract attention, especially if you raise large amounts through crowdfunding platforms or use nonprofit labels without a 501(c)(3).

To stay safe:

- Use personal accounts with clear labels like "rent help" or "utilities."

- Avoid using words like "salary," "stipend," or "pay" unless it is accurate.

- Keep amounts small and direct.

- Use decentralized tools like Cash App, Venmo, PayPal Friends and Family, or physical gift cards.

- If you build a fund, consider a rotating coordinator instead of a formal treasurer.

Large cash transfers over ten thousand dollars may be reported to the IRS. Keep records clear. Platforms like Venmo may flag large or suspicious transactions. Use "Friends and Family" for small amounts. If you go public, keep public records clean and transparent. State clearly where the money is going and avoid promising things you cannot verify or deliver.

Harm Reduction and First Aid: What Is Allowed

You are allowed to carry Narcan. You are allowed to give someone water and a snack during a crisis. You can legally hand someone a first aid kit or bandages. You can sit with them while they come down from a high.

Where it gets tricky:

- Distributing controlled substances.

- Providing injections of any kind.

- Acting as medical personnel without certification.

If you run a harm reduction station, do not claim medical status unless you are licensed. It is usually legal to distribute clean syringes and test strips, but this varies by state. Check www.harmreduction.org for your state's laws or partner with a group that already knows the rules.

How to Handle Police or City Complaints

If someone calls the city or police on your operation:

- Stay calm. Do not argue.

- Ask if you are being cited or warned. Get it in writing.

- Record the interaction if it is legal in your state.

- If you are told to leave, do it peacefully and regroup elsewhere.

Record interactions in one-party consent states. In two-party states like California, get consent or do not record audio. Your best protection is quiet success. If you serve people without disturbing traffic, drawing attention, or claiming political territory, you are much harder to shut down.

Document everything. Have a phone tree. Know who your local civil rights lawyers are. Be ready to shift tactics if visibility becomes a liability.

Final Word

Helping people should not be dangerous. But in a society built around control and scarcity, real solidarity looks like rebellion.

You do not need to stop. You just need to adapt. Keep your operations tight. Protect your people. Stay off the radar when possible. Go public only when the cost is worth it.

They cannot stop mutual aid. But they will try to scare you out of doing it. That is how you know it matters.

Resources That Might Help:

- www.harmreduction.org for harm reduction laws and supplies.
- www.nlg.org for legal support during raids or citations.
- www.mutualaiddisasterrelief.org for mutual aid networks and training.
- www.municode.com for checking local ordinances.
- www.nolo.com for legal consent laws.
- www.optoutprescreen.com to reduce exposure to data

brokers.

- Partner with 501(c)(3) groups to access permits or legal protection.

- Use trusted platforms like GoFundMe and verify recipients before donating or fundraising.

Chapter 15: Guerrilla Infrastructure

When the System Fails, You Build Your Own

Some people wait years for help that never comes. Others give up entirely, deciding to live without water, power, or stability. A third group quietly builds their own systems. They fix what they can. They work around what they cannot. They share what they learn.

This chapter is about those people. Not off-grid survivalists or doomsday cultists, just regular people who decided to stop waiting and start wiring, fixing, storing, or building for themselves and their neighbors.

Guerrilla infrastructure fills gaps during utility shutoffs, evictions, or disasters when systems fail. While often necessary, these actions may violate local zoning or health codes. Know the risks before you act.

What Is Guerrilla Infrastructure?

Guerrilla infrastructure means creating or restoring access to essential needs—power, water, shelter, waste handling—without waiting for official permission or centralized systems.

Examples include:

- Charging phones off car batteries.
- Collecting rainwater to flush toilets.
- Running power tools off solar panels or inverters.
- Building tiny shelters on land no one wants.

- Setting up shared laundry or hot water systems in informal housing.

It is not about escaping society. It is about surviving when the system is broken or unwilling to help.

Power: Charging, Storing, and Staying Online

Even a little electricity can change everything. It keeps lights on, devices charged, food cold, and communication possible.

Basic tools that work:

- Portable battery packs, especially those with solar panels, costing around $20–$100.

- Car inverters that turn a cigarette lighter into a power source.

- Used solar panels wired to charge twelve-volt batteries. Always follow guides from reliable sources like www.solarpowerworldonline.com.

- Power stations like Jackery or EcoFlow, starting around $200.

If your electricity is shut off:

- Use local libraries, gyms, or churches to charge devices.

- Ask friends to run extension cords through windows.

- Use car batteries to power small LED lights or phone chargers.

- Avoid space heaters or hot plates on improvised setups due to fire risk.

Most guerrilla power setups are short-term. That is fine. You only need enough to bridge the gap or keep a household functional until the next break.

Water: What You Can Store, Purify, or Capture

Without running water, everything gets harder. Toilets stop working. Cooking becomes dangerous. Hygiene collapses fast.

Here is what helps:

- Five-gallon buckets with lids for water storage.

- Gravity-fed filters like Berkey or Sawyer for drinking water.

- Rain barrels if you have roof access or a yard. Check www.nrdc.org for state laws on rainwater collection.

- Bleach or purification tablets to make emergency sources drinkable. Use eight drops of unscented bleach per gallon of clear water.

- Milk jugs filled ahead of time stored in closets or under beds.

If you are in a place with frequent shutoffs, always have a backup supply. Even a single fifty-five-gallon barrel can buy you a week of safety.

Shelter: Where to Sleep When No One Will House You

This is the hardest and most legally dangerous part of guerrilla living. Cities criminalize homelessness while refusing to build housing. That leaves people with few options.

Survival strategies:

- Tiny homes on trailers parked on private property or rotating lots. Check www.tinyhomeindustryassociation.org for legal guidance.

- Converted vans or cars with insulation, reflectors, and fans.

- Tents with weatherproofing and heating pads powered by battery packs.

- Shared spaces with staggered schedules where people sleep in shifts.

If you are sheltering people informally:

- Keep numbers low and quiet.

- Avoid high-visibility zones.

- Partner with churches or landowners who are sympathetic.

- Rotate locations when needed to avoid burnout or legal attention.

You do not need to build permanence. You need to build protection.

Heat, Sanitation, and Waste

People think of infrastructure as power lines and pipes. But the basics are smaller: warmth, hygiene, and clean surroundings.

Heat options:

- USB or battery-powered heating pads.

- Tea light heaters made from ceramic pots. Never leave

these unattended.

- Mylar blankets for insulation.
- Layered clothing and shared sleeping zones.

Sanitation:

- Camp toilets or five-gallon buckets with sawdust or kitty litter. Dispose of waste according to local health codes.
- Hand sanitizer and wet wipes in bulk.
- Vinegar spray and bleach for disinfection.
- Public restrooms, gyms, and parks as fallback options.

You are not trying to recreate a full utility grid. You are trying to stay alive and keep people from getting sick. Small things make a huge difference.

When to Stay Invisible, and When to Go Loud

Most guerrilla infrastructure efforts stay quiet. That is not cowardice. It is protection. Public attention can bring support, but it also brings police, zoning inspectors, and code enforcement.

If you are:

- Housing people in trailers.
- Running a food-sharing fridge.
- Hosting community showers or clinics.

You should assume city attention is coming eventually.

If you are:

- Charging your neighbor's devices.

- Letting someone sleep in a van.
- Catching rain in a barrel.

You may never be noticed, unless someone complains.

Partner with nonprofits or local community organizations when possible. Choose visibility when you have backup. Stay quiet when you are vulnerable. Learn from both.

Final Word

When people say "just get help," they forget that the help already failed. You are not building these systems because you want to play hero. You are building them because the official systems gave up.

There is no shame in fixing what the state will not. There is only risk and only if you are visible. Work with care. Share what works. Help without asking for permission.

Every shelter, every socket, every gallon of clean water you create is one less person broken by the system.

Additional Resources:

- www.mutualaiddisasterrelief.org for mutual aid collaboration.
- www.nlg.org for legal support.
- www.harmreduction.org for harm reduction guidelines.
- www.instructables.com and DIY YouTube channels for safe setups.

- www.nrdc.org for rainwater collection laws.

- www.tinyhomeindustryassociation.org for tiny home regulations.

Beware of scams. Use trusted retailers like Amazon or REI for equipment. Verify all laws locally before starting.

Chapter 16: The Real Rules of Protest

Some protests make history. Most do not.

That is not because the cause is weak. It is because organizers fail to understand the terrain, the risks, and the real rules.

This chapter is not about ideology. It is about survival. If you put your body in the street, you need to know exactly what you are walking into. These are the real rules of protest in the United States—based on law, lived experience, and what happens when the cameras leave.

You Have the Right to Protest Until They Say You Do Not

The First Amendment protects:

- The right to assemble
- The right to express political beliefs
- The right to record public officials in public spaces

These rights are real. They are also conditional. Police often override them with curfews, "unlawful assembly" declarations, or local ordinances. Once a gathering is declared unlawful, your rights narrow fast.

Courts have upheld time, place, and manner restrictions. This means the government can limit protests with curfews, permit requirements, or noise rules if applied equally.

"Unlawful assembly" is a vague term that police often use to justify dispersal. They may claim disorder, risk of violence, or public inconvenience. You have fewer rights once this is declared.

Recording police in public is protected under federal case law, including *Glik v. Cunniffe* (2011), but some states may interfere. Always check current guidance from the ACLU at www.aclu.org.

Do not assume your constitutional rights will protect you in the moment. They may help later in court. If your goal is to avoid arrest or injury, learn to read the situation before it escalates.

Know the Risk Before You Show Up

Before you attend a protest, ask:

- Is this a permitted or unpermitted action?
- Who is organizing?
- What is the stated goal?
- How have police responded at similar events in this city?

Permitted protests usually require formal applications to the city. Unpermitted actions may carry a higher risk of police response.

A family-friendly march at noon with a permit is not the same as a midnight freeway blockade. Do not trust social media fliers. Talk to people who have been at past protests in the area.

If you are undocumented, on probation, or have active warrants, do not attend unless you fully understand the risks. Police often use attendance alone as a pretext for detention.

You can check local protest history using ACLU archives or local news.

What to Bring and What to Leave at Home

Bring:

- Water
- ID, unless you are intentionally protecting your identity
- A written emergency contact number
- A bandana soaked in vinegar or sealed goggles for tear gas
- Earplugs if sound weapons are likely
- A marker to write jail support numbers on your arm
- Snacks and a phone stripped of personal data

Carrying ID may speed up your release but could expose your identity if you are undocumented or have legal concerns. Weigh the risk.

Do not bring:

- Weapons or illegal substances
- Anything illegal, even by mistake
- Contact lenses if tear gas is a possibility
- Phones with personal data or active GPS tracking

Encrypt your phone and disable cloud backups before attending. If your phone is seized, encrypted data and disabled syncing protect your information.

Dress plainly. Cover tattoos. Wear neutral clothing and durable shoes. The goal is to avoid being singled out or later identified by facial recognition.

Tear Gas, Rubber Bullets, and Crowd Control

Police do not have to warn you before using force. They may fire tear gas or begin kettling—a tactic where they trap groups inside police lines before arresting everyone.

If tear gas is deployed:

- Move laterally out of the cloud. Do not run blindly.
- Cover your mouth and nose with a cloth soaked in vinegar or lemon juice.
- Flush your eyes with water or saline, not milk.
- Seek medical attention if exposure causes lasting symptoms.
- Do not rub your face or wear oil-based products.

Kettling is controversial and has been the subject of lawsuits, including *Black Lives Matter v. Trump* (2020). If you are trapped, remain calm and contact legal aid after release.

If hit with rubber bullets, pepper balls, or bean bags:

- Get medical attention immediately. These weapons cause serious injuries.
- Document your injury and, if possible, the officer involved.
- Do not expect apologies. Get treatment and legal help if needed.

Arrest, Jail, and What Happens Next

If arrested:

- Say, "I am invoking my right to remain silent. I want a lawyer." Then say nothing else.

- Do not argue or explain.

- Do not sign anything without reading and understanding it.

- Expect to be held for several hours or overnight.

Jail support teams often monitor large protests. They:

- Track arrests

- Wait outside the jail for release

- Provide water, food, and transport

Write the jail support number on your arm. Tell a trusted person your plans before attending.

If you are released with a charge, show up to every court date. If you are released without paperwork, check your mail for follow-up. Public defenders and legal aid groups can help. Contact www.lsc.gov/find-legal-aid if needed.

How to Protect Other Protesters

If you are less likely to be targeted, use that position to protect others:

- Stand between police and vulnerable protesters when it is safe to do so

- Record events openly and clearly

- Avoid posting faces or names of protesters online, especially minors or undocumented individuals

- Share supplies, rides, and food with people in the crowd

Protest is about protecting each other, not about spectacle or personal gain. Use your presence to create safety.

Use encrypted apps like Signal for organizing and communicating with protest groups.

What Actually Creates Pressure

A protest without follow-up achieves little. Real pressure comes from:

- Coordinated, specific demands
- Disruption of economic or political systems
- Legal action and exposure of official misconduct
- Ongoing engagement with press, supporters, and legislators

If a protest ends and no action follows, the system resets. Marches are only tools. They are not a strategy by themselves.

Police surveillance is constant. Expect body cameras, drones, and social media monitoring. Assume anything you post can be used against you.

Final Word

You do not have to march to make change. But if you do, know the stakes. Know how to protect yourself and others. Know what you are trying to accomplish.

The streets are not sacred ground. They are contested space. If you show up, show up ready.

Chapter 17: Jail Support, Bail Funds, and Getting Out Clean

The protest is not over when the cops show up. It just moves to a different room.

Once arrests begin, everything changes. The people who stood in the street become detainees in a system that treats protest as a crime and dissent as a threat.

This chapter is not about theory. It is about what really happens after the arrest and how to help someone caught in it, or how to help yourself if it is your turn.

What Jail Support Actually Means

Jail support happens outside the cell. It means:

- Tracking who was arrested
- Waiting at the jail for their release
- Bringing food, water, and a phone charger
- Helping with paperwork
- Making sure no one walks out alone or into danger

Jail support often involves coordinating with legal aid or bail funds, such as those connected to the National Lawyers Guild (www.nlg.org). Volunteers doing jail support should avoid arrest themselves to remain available.

You do not need to be a lawyer or an activist. You just have to show up, take notes, and wait. Sometimes it takes an hour. Sometimes it takes all night.

Before the Arrest: What to Do in Advance

If you are joining a protest where arrests are likely:

- Write a jail support number on your arm with permanent marker

- Tell a friend where you are going and what you are wearing

- Carry an ID if you feel safe doing so

- Bring essential medications in labeled containers with a prescription—unlabeled drugs may be denied in custody

- Do not carry anything that could raise charges—tools, knives, or even certain protest signs

- Encrypt your phone and disable cloud backups before attending

If you are running jail support for others:

- Start a shared spreadsheet with attendees, legal names if possible, and emergency contacts

- Set up a group chat for tracking arrests and releases

- Coordinate with local lawyers or bail funds ahead of time

Preparation is the difference between chaos and control.

During the Arrest: What to Expect

If police begin making arrests:

- You may be zip-tied or cuffed

- You will probably be searched and transported to central

booking

- Your phone may be taken. Lock it first or leave it behind

Stay calm. Do not resist unless you make a strategic decision to do so. Resisting arrest may add charges like obstruction. Weigh that risk carefully. Say:

"I am remaining silent. I want a lawyer."

Repeat it if needed. Say nothing else about your identity, intentions, or group beyond what is legally required for booking.

After the Arrest: Inside the System

Once inside the jail, expect:

- Another search
- Fingerprinting and booking
- Time in a holding cell

Depending on the charge and the city, you may:

- Be released that night on your own recognizance
- Be held until arraignment
- Be assigned bail

Holding times vary by jurisdiction, from 4 to 48 hours before arraignment. If you cannot afford a lawyer, request a public defender at your arraignment.

One call, one person waiting outside, or someone tracking your case can mean the difference between a quick release and a long ordeal.

Bail Funds: How They Work and Why They Matter

Bail is not a fine. It is a deposit to guarantee your return to court. If you miss court, the money is gone. If you show up, the money is refunded, sometimes with court fees deducted.

Bail funds exist to:

- Reduce harm from pretrial detention

- Keep people from losing jobs, housing, or custody

- Stop the system from isolating individuals

Bail amounts vary widely. For protest-related charges, bail can range from $500 to $10,000 depending on the jurisdiction and charges. Some states have reduced or eliminated cash bail—check www.aclu.org for your local laws.

Check www.nationalbailout.org to find a bail fund near you. Most cities have at least one. Some focus on protests, others on marginalized communities. They often work with defense lawyers or direct action groups.

If you need help from a bail fund, contact them with:

- The legal name of the person arrested

- The time and place of arrest

- Known charges

- The jail's location if known

Never post arrest details publicly without permission. Always protect the person's safety first.

Getting Out Clean: What to Do After Release

When someone is released, they are usually:

- Disoriented
- Hungry
- Exhausted
- Still in the clothes they were arrested in
- Unclear about their next court date

Good support means:

- Meeting them when they walk out
- Giving them food, water, and a charger
- Getting them home or somewhere safe
- Helping them write down what happened before memories fade
- Taking photos of injuries if needed

Remind them:

- Court dates are not optional
- Paperwork may still come by mail
- Legal help is available (www.lsc.gov/find-legal-aid)
- They are not alone

If you are the one arrested, do the same for yourself. Write it all down. Contact legal aid. Do not let shame or exhaustion stop you from protecting yourself.

Police may monitor social media or use facial recognition after a protest. Be cautious about what you post.

Final Word

Jail support is protest without a sign. Bail funds are resistance without a chant.

If you cannot march, run jail support. If you cannot risk arrest, track court dates. If you cannot give money, give your time.

When the system tries to disappear people, these are the tools that bring them back into the light.

Chapter 18: What They Really Mean by "Justice"

It Sounds Noble. It Looks Fair. But It Works Like a Machine.

Most Americans grow up believing justice is blind. We are taught if you follow the law, speak respectfully, and wait your turn, the system will protect you. But once you fall into it—whether through a traffic stop, a custody fight, or a petty arrest—you learn the truth. The system does not protect you. It processes you.

The word "justice" has been hollowed out. It is stamped on courthouse doors and prosecutor letterheads. But in practice, it usually means punishment, delay, and submission.

This chapter is not about theory. It is about how the idea of justice got turned into a weapon and how that matters when you are fighting to survive inside its shell.

The System Is Built to Convict Not Understand

Public defenders in the U.S. routinely carry 100 to 300 cases at a time, often leaving them unable to dedicate meaningful attention to any single client. Prosecutors may be rewarded with promotions or political backing based on high conviction rates, valuing wins over fairness. Judges are elected or appointed by politicians who campaign on "tough on crime" platforms, making them sensitive to public pressure for harsh sentences.

Your guilt or innocence is not their priority. The priority is clearing the docket. You will be pressured to accept a plea. You will be warned not to fight. If you resist, you risk harsher outcomes for slowing the machine down.

This is not a mistake. It is how the system is designed to run.

Who Gets Justice Depends on What You Look Like and What You Can Pay

Justice flows based on income, skin color, neighborhood, and perceived social value.

- Wealthy defendants can hire private lawyers, post bail, and negotiate terms.
- Poor defendants often get overwhelmed public defenders and are pushed toward plea deals.
- White defendants may benefit from subconscious bias.
- Black Americans are incarcerated at five times the rate of whites and often receive longer sentences for similar charges.

Even in the same courthouse, two people facing the same charge can have radically different outcomes based on race, wealth, or even how they are dressed.

The scales of justice are not broken. They are tilted by design.

"Innocent Until Proven Guilty" Is a Slogan, Not a Shield

About half a million people sit in U.S. jails every day awaiting trial, not because they were convicted, but because they could not afford bail. Pretrial detention varies by state—places like California and New York have reduced cash bail—but in many jurisdictions, sitting in jail before trial is standard.

You can lose your housing, your job, your custody rights, and your mental health while waiting for a hearing that may be rescheduled five times. Even if you are acquitted, the damage is often permanent.

This is not justice. It is containment.

The Plea Deal Trap

Between 94% and 97% of criminal cases in the United States end with a plea deal. Most people never get a trial.

Defendants are told, "If you take this deal today, you can go home." So some plead guilty even when they are innocent. Some plea deals, like Alford pleas, allow defendants to plead guilty while maintaining their innocence.

That plea will follow you for life—blocking housing, employment, education, custody rights, and travel. The system does not care. It got a conviction. It closed the file.

This is what justice looks like in practice: speed, pressure, and body counts.

Courtrooms Are About Control, Not Truth

Every aspect of courtroom behavior—how you speak, how you stand, how you address the judge—is designed to remind you who holds power.

If you fail to follow the script, you can be held in contempt of court, which may result in fines or jail time depending on state law. Evidence may be ignored. Testimony may be dismissed. But rolling your eyes, speaking out of turn, or failing to say "Your Honor" can land you in more trouble than the facts of your case.

This is about control, not fairness.

Know the rules of the stage you are standing on. Follow them when it serves you. Challenge them only when you understand the risks.

When "Justice" Just Means Survival

For most people, "justice" means surviving the system with as little damage as possible. That might mean taking a bad deal to avoid prison. Sitting silently through endless continuances. Walking out of court knowing you were right and still lost.

Survival is not justice. But sometimes, it is the only goal that makes sense.

If You Are Facing the System: What You Should Know

- **Some states have reduced cash bail.** Check www.aclu.org for local rules.

- **Some convictions can be expunged.** Contact Legal Aid to see if your record can be cleared.

- **Community support matters.** Groups like www.nlg.org offer court support and advocacy.

Final Word

If you still believe in justice, that is not naïve. It is memory.

Once, there was a vision of fairness and accountability. But the system you live in today is not that vision. It is a machine built on fear, compliance, and conviction rates.

Knowing this is not giving up. It is waking up.

You can still fight. You can still help others fight. You can still carve out moments of truth in a wrecked system. But do not confuse their slogans for your values.

Their justice is not your justice.

Chapter 19: How to Spot a Trap When They Call It "Help"

Not Every Hand Offered Is There to Lift You Up

Some programs sound generous but are structured to fail. Some offers of help come laced with surveillance, control tactics, or conditions so harsh they leave you worse off. Some people and agencies offer a way out but use your desperation as leverage.

This chapter is about spotting traps disguised as help. It is not about rejecting every offer or distrusting everyone. It is about knowing how power works, especially when it smiles.

The Five Signs of a Trap

1. Help That Requires You to Give Up Rights

Some programs demand you:

- Sign away your right to sue.
- Waive confidentiality.
- Accept police supervision.
- Agree to random drug tests or inspections.

These are not safety measures. They are control tactics. Always ask what rights you give up in exchange. If you cannot say no without punishment, it is not help, it is leverage.

2. Help That Comes With Surveillance

If a program requires you to:

- Install tracking apps.

- Check in constantly.
- Report daily behaviors.

It may be gathering more than just progress updates. Those data points can be sold, shared, or used against you in custody fights, court cases, or eviction hearings.

Always ask:

- Who gets access?
- What is stored?
- What happens if I stop participating?

3. **Help That Ends When You Show Progress**

Some programs punish you the second you improve. You make a little money, and the help disappears.

Watch for:

- Income cliffs that cut off Medicaid or food stamps.
- Subsidies that vanish after one paycheck.
- Vouchers that only apply if you stay unemployed.

Real help builds a bridge. Fake help collapses under you the moment you take a step.

4. **Help That Demands Unpaid Labor or Loyalty**

Some programs expect you to:

- "Volunteer" as a condition of getting help.
- Attend religious services or therapy sessions.
- Promote their group on social media.

- Stay silent about mistreatment.

Help is not supposed to be a transaction. If the cost is your time, your silence, or your loyalty, you are being used.

5. **Help That Cuts You Off From Others**

Be wary of services that:

- Discourage outside contact.

- Ban visitors or family.

- Restrict phone use.

- Tell you not to talk to a lawyer.

Real support does not isolate. It connects.

Government Programs Built to Fail

Some traps are baked into law:

- Work requirements with no real jobs.

- Reentry programs without housing.

- Emergency aid that shows up three months too late.

- "Community policing" that spies on you instead of helping.

These programs exist to lower statistics, win funding, or make agencies look good, not to solve problems. You can use them. Just do it with your eyes open. Take what you need. Leave before they take more than they give.

What Real Help Looks Like

Real help:

- Is offered without coercion.

- Gives you full information up front.

- Respects your decisions.

- Does not ask for performance or gratitude.

If you have to act grateful or prove your worth to get it, that is not help. That is control.

Questions to Ask Before You Say Yes

- What do I have to give up?

- What happens if I stop?

- Who is watching me, and why?

- What are the long-term consequences?

- Would I recommend this to someone I love?

If you would not want it for someone you care about, do not take it blindly just because you are tired or desperate. Exhaustion is the hook these systems count on.

Final Word

Sometimes the system fails you by accident. Sometimes by design. And sometimes it offers you a lifeline that is just tight enough to choke you.

This chapter is not telling you to stop seeking help. It is telling you to protect your agency while doing it. Use what works. Walk away from what doesn't. Stay alert. Trust patterns.

The help you need is out there. But you may have to step over a few traps to find it.

Chapter 20: The System Is Working Exactly as Designed

If the Goal Were to Help You, It Would Look Very Different

Every time you wait hours in line, get denied for a missing form you were never sent, or lose housing over a technicality, someone says the same thing: "The system is broken."

It is not broken. It is doing what it was built to do.

This chapter is not a conspiracy theory. It is a reality check. The system's paperwork, delays, threats, and confusion are intentional because those outcomes benefit the people in charge. What you are experiencing is not an accident. It is policy in motion.

Designed to Delay, Not Deliver

The longer it takes you to access food, housing, or healthcare, the fewer people will try. That cuts costs for the state and creates the illusion of scarcity. If they say the money ran out, it sounds like bad luck. If you say the website never loaded, it sounds like your problem.

Bureaucracy is a filter. It weeds out people who give up. The system was not built to reach everyone. It was built to reduce how many people it helps.

Designed to Punish Before You're Guilty

You do not have to be convicted of a crime to lose your freedom. You do not have to break a law to be investigated, harassed, or evicted.

Pretrial detention. Child welfare investigations. Public housing inspections. These are not neutral safety checks. They are surveillance mechanisms used to control poor people, disabled people, mentally ill people, and politically inconvenient people.

The message is clear: stay compliant or lose what little you have. That is not justice. That is enforcement.

Designed to Humiliate You Into Silence

If you have ever had to beg for rent help, explain your trauma to strangers, or prove your disability in front of a panel, you know most systems are designed to humble you.

The more you have to perform gratitude or desperation, the less likely you are to fight back. That is the point. Shame makes you quiet. Bureaucracy makes you tired.

Together, they keep you in line.

Designed to Blame You When It Fails

When benefits do not arrive, the housing list closes, or the helpline never picks up, the system does not apologize. It blames you.

You missed the form. You missed the deadline. You did not follow the rules.

By making every failure look personal, the system avoids accountability. The error is never theirs. It is always yours.

That is not broken logic. That is self-defense written into policy.

124

What Would a Real System Look Like?

If the system were designed to help people, it would:

- Minimize steps, not multiply them.

- Offer help without surveillance.

- Provide second chances, not permanent punishments.

- Reward honesty, not performance.

- Run on realistic timelines, not red tape.

If that sounds naïve, it is only because we have been trained to expect dysfunction. Most people do not expect fairness. They expect delay, suspicion, and dismissal.

That is not a policy failure. That is a moral failure.

Final Word

You are not struggling because you are lazy.

You are not stuck because you are stupid.

You are not falling through the cracks. You were pushed.

If it feels like you are fighting a machine, that is because you are. And that machine was built to outlast complaints, ignore the poor, and punish the honest.

Once you see it for what it is, you stop blaming yourself. You start fighting smarter. And you realize this was never about you. It was always structural.

Now you have a map.

If You Are Facing This System: What You Should Know

- **Some states have reduced or eliminated cash bail.** Check www.aclu.org for updates.

- **Use www.lsc.gov/find-legal-aid for free legal help.** They assist with housing, benefits, and appeals.

- **Some convictions and evictions can be sealed or expunged.** Legal Aid can help you clear your record.

- **Data from government aid applications may be shared with law enforcement or sold to private companies.** Check www.eff.org for digital privacy tips.

- **Community groups like www.nlg.org offer advocacy and court support.**

Questions to Ask Before You Accept Help

- What rights am I giving up?

- Who will have access to my data, and for how long?

- What happens if I stop participating?

- What are the long-term consequences?

- Would I recommend this to someone I care about?

Do not assume they are on your side. Protect yourself before you step in.

Chapter 21: How to Avoid Getting Cut Off After Approval

They Gave It to You Once. That Doesn't Mean They Want You to Keep It.

Getting approved for benefits is hard. Keeping them can be harder. Agencies do not forget about you once they send the money. They monitor you. They flag files. And they regularly conduct reviews to thin the list.

This chapter covers how people lose access to food stamps, Medicaid, disability income, or housing—often through no fault of their own—and what you can do to protect yourself once you're finally in the system.

Why They Cut People Off

It is rarely fraud. In fact, fraud causes less than 2% of SNAP terminations. Most cuts happen because:

- You missed a paperwork deadline.
- They mailed a letter you never got.
- They claim your income went up when it didn't.
- A system flag triggered an automated suspension.
- A review got skipped, and the file was closed.

"Data matching" often compares your file to federal records like IRS or SSA databases but these can contain errors that falsely flag income changes. The system does not need to prove you did something wrong. It just needs an excuse to stop paying.

Common Programs and How They Drop You

SNAP (Food stamps):

- Requires re-certification every 6–12 months.

- Miss the interview or fail to submit income forms and you're cut.

- Many states offer re-certification by phone—check www.fns.usda.gov/snap.

- Changes in household composition can trigger immediate review.

Medicaid:

- Periodic renewals restarted in most states after COVID.

- States use data matching with IRS or employer records.

- Some states auto-renew Medicaid if data matches— confirm with www.medicaid.gov.

- One missed letter can mean sudden ineligibility.

SSI/SSDI (Disability):

- Reviewed every 3–7 years.

- Reviews demand new medical proof—gather doctor letters early.

- Any side income over $1,550/month (2025) can trigger suspension.

- Overpayments often come from agency errors.

Housing Assistance (Section 8, Public Housing):

- Annual reviews are mandatory.

- Changes in household income, guests, or employment must be reported.

- Landlords can also trigger reevaluation.

What to Do When You Get a Review Notice

Do not ignore it. Respond on time even if you don't have all the documents yet.

If you need more time:

- Call and ask.

- Submit partial paperwork.

- Write a letter explaining delays.

Always ask for written confirmation that they received your materials. File SNAP or Medicaid appeals within 10–15 days to keep benefits active—check your notice for exact deadlines. If they deny your renewal, appeal immediately.

How to Avoid Unintentional Triggers

- Update your contact info with every agency as soon as it changes.

- Use online portals like SSA.gov or state platforms like BenefitsCal.

- Check your mail weekly even if you hate doing it.

- Save copies of every form you submit.

- Report income changes promptly, even if minor.

- Keep all re-certification dates on a calendar with reminders.

If you receive Medicaid or SNAP, call them every six months even if you get no letters. Ask if any actions are needed to keep your case active.

When They Claim You Were Overpaid

Overpayments are often the agency's mistake. Do not panic.

- Ask for a full explanation of how the overpayment was calculated.

- Request a copy of your file.

- Appeal immediately.

- If the overpayment is valid, request a repayment plan or waiver.

- Request a waiver if repayment would cause financial hardship—see www.ssa.gov for SSI/SSDI.

Never agree to repay without understanding where the numbers came from. Never ignore a repayment demand—that can trigger collections, wage garnishment, or benefit suspension.

Final Word

Approval is not safety. You are still in the system and the system is designed to be temporary, even when your need is permanent.

Stay alert. Stay organized. Keep the pipeline open. And never assume silence means security.

If You Need Help Navigating the System

- Some states auto-renew SNAP and Medicaid if data matches—confirm at www.medicaid.gov.

- Contact www.nlg.org for help with unfair terminations or overpayment disputes.

- Some states eased SNAP work requirements after 2023—check www.fns.usda.gov for updates.

- Use www.lsc.gov/find-legal-aid for free legal help with benefits, housing, and appeals.

Chapter 22: When You Can Tell a Cop to Leave, and When You Can't

They Don't Always Need a Warrant. But You Don't Always Have to Let Them In.

Knowing when to assert your rights without escalating the situation can be the difference between going to bed and going to jail. It can also be the difference between keeping your home intact and watching it get searched without justification.

This chapter is about understanding the real rules of police entry—what you can say, what they can do, and when you have to comply.

First Question: Are You Inside or Outside?

The Constitution protects your home more than any other location. Once you step outside, your rights shrink. The moment a cop is at your door, what you say next matters.

- If you are outside your home or in public, you do not control the space.

- If you are inside and they are knocking, you are under no obligation to open the door unless they have a warrant or valid exception.

Do not open the door unless you know why they are there. Speak through a window or closed door if needed. This is legal. It is also safer.

Police may also use "knock-and-talk" tactics—knocking and asking for consent to enter without a warrant. You can say no.

Do They Have a Warrant?

Ask this directly and clearly: "Do you have a warrant?"

If the answer is yes:

- Ask to see it through the window or screen door.

- Read the name, address, and scope. Is it for your residence? Is your name on it?

- A valid warrant lists your address, your name, or specific items to be searched. If it is for someone else, it may not apply to you.

- A warrant for your neighbor, roommate, or someone else does not give them access to your space.

If the answer is no:

- Say, "I do not consent to any search."

- Then stay silent.

If they claim they do not need a warrant, they are claiming an exception and you need to know what those are.

The Four Main Exceptions to the Warrant Rule

Consent:
If you say yes, they can come in. Most illegal searches happen because someone gave permission without realizing they had the power to say no.

Exigent Circumstances:
If an officer believes someone is in immediate danger, evidence is being destroyed, or a serious crime is occurring, they can enter without a warrant. They must justify this later in court. Document

their stated reason.

Plain View:

If illegal items are visible through a window or open door, police may enter to secure the evidence but only if they are legally present outside. Keep your space private and your doors closed.

Arrests:

If someone is being arrested inside, police can enter to complete the arrest and perform a limited safety sweep.

Common Situations and What You Can Legally Do

Situation: You hear a knock and see a uniform.

- Do not open the door until you ask who they are and why they are there.

- Ask if they have a warrant.

- If they do not, say, "I do not consent to any entry or search."

Situation: They say they are doing a welfare check.

- Ask, "Am I being accused of anything?"

- If you are okay, say, "I am safe and do not require assistance. I do not consent to any search."

- You may decline a welfare check unless they can prove an immediate threat.

Situation: You are on probation or parole.

- Your rights may be limited.

- Check your probation terms. Some allow home searches

without a warrant.

- Probation search rules vary by state—check your agreement or call www.lsc.gov/find-legal-aid.

- If unsure, call your supervising officer before letting police in.

Situation: They are aggressive or threatening arrest.

- Stay calm.

- Do not physically block them if they force entry.

- Say clearly, "I do not consent to this search."

- Remain silent and document everything later with a lawyer.

- In one-party consent states, you may be able to legally record interactions—check www.nolo.com for your state laws.

What If It's Someone Else's Space?

If you live with others:

- You cannot consent to a search of someone else's private room.

- They cannot consent to a search of your locked space or personal belongings.

- Common areas (like the living room) are vulnerable if one roommate gives consent.

If you are a guest:

- You have no right to block entry unless your personal

belongings are being searched.

If you are the tenant and police want to enter someone else's rented room:

- You may say, "That room belongs to someone else and I do not have authority to allow access."

Final Word

You are allowed to say no.

You are allowed to close the door.

You are allowed to make the police do their job by the book.

You will not win every time. But the more you understand the rules, the harder it is for them to break them without consequence.

Say no. Stay calm. Record what you can. Police may use body cams or drones—cover identifiable features and document their actions. If they search without a valid warrant, contact www.nlg.org for legal help.

Warrant rules may vary slightly by state—check www.nolo.com for local laws. If they want to come inside, they need a legal reason and you are not required to give them one.

Chapter 23: Unemployment — What They Don't Tell You Until You're Denied

It's Not a Handout. It's Insurance You Already Paid Into.

Most people don't know how unemployment works until they lose a job and get hit with silence, denial, or confusing demands for documents they've never seen before.

This chapter explains how Unemployment Insurance (UI) actually works, who qualifies, why denials happen, and how to fight back when the system tries to shut you out.

What Unemployment Insurance Actually Is

Unemployment isn't welfare. It's a state-run insurance program funded by federal and state payroll taxes your employer already paid. If you lose your job through no fault of your own, the system is supposed to provide temporary cash while you look for work.

UI benefits typically range from $235 to $823 per week for up to 26 weeks, depending on your state.

In theory:

- You apply after being laid off, fired without cause, or forced to quit due to unsafe or hostile conditions.

- You report weekly or biweekly that you're still unemployed and able to work.

- The state sends you a check.

In practice: It's a bureaucratic maze that delays, denies, and punishes anyone who doesn't follow the hidden script.

Who Actually Qualifies

To get UI, you usually must:

- Have earned enough wages in your "base period" (usually the first four of the last five completed quarters).

- Be unemployed through no fault of your own.

- Be able and available to work.

- Actively look for work and submit proof (unless waived).

Laid off? You probably qualify.

Fired for misconduct? It depends and they have to prove it. Denials often claim "misconduct" without providing evidence. Always request specific proof if you appeal.

Quit? You may still qualify if it was for good cause, like unsafe conditions, harassment, or unpaid wages but you'll need to explain and prove it. Good cause rules vary by state.

Why They Deny People So Often

States are often financially motivated to keep approval rates low and delay payments. Common tactics include:

- Claiming you didn't earn enough in your base period.

- Saying your separation was "voluntary."

- Demanding proof of job searches in a broken portal.

- Flagging you for fraud based on faulty data.

Denial letters are often vague, with only a code or legal phrase.

How to Appeal a Denial

Every state has an appeals process. Use it.

You usually have 10–30 days to request a hearing, which is often a phone call with an administrative judge.

Say: "I want to appeal this denial and request a hearing. I disagree with the decision and can provide additional documentation."

Bring:

- Pay stubs, W-2s.

- Separation notices.

- Emails or texts showing your termination or resignation reasons.

- Screenshots of job searches (if required).

Winning an appeal may restore benefits retroactively, so file on time.

What to Know About Overpayments and Fraud Flags

Sometimes they pay you for weeks, then claim you were never eligible and demand the money back. This is called an overpayment.

- Some overpayments are their fault (agency error).

- Some are yours (reporting mistakes, etc.).

- Either way, many states allow you to request a waiver, especially if repayment would cause hardship.

Fraud accusations are worse. They can be triggered by:

- A mismatch in employer-reported data.

- Typing errors in your application.

- Outdated ID verification systems.

Fraud penalties may include fines or benefit bans. Always respond in writing. Demand proof. You are entitled to a hearing before they can collect.

Pandemic Hangover: Why It Got Worse

During COVID, expanded UI programs paid people who wouldn't normally qualify (like gig workers and the self-employed). When those programs ended, many states started clawing money back—usually from the poorest and most vulnerable, not from fraudsters.

If you get a "pandemic overpayment" letter:

- Don't panic.

- Ask for a waiver.

- Some states still offer PUA overpayment waivers—check www.dol.gov.

- Get legal aid if you can.

Final Word

Unemployment isn't charity. You earned it.

But they'll still make you feel like a criminal for applying.

File anyway. Appeal denials. Keep your documentation. Don't trust their website to be current. Never assume a rejection is final.

You didn't fail. The system is designed to wear you down.
Push back.

Tips for Navigating the System

- Use state UI portals (e.g., EDD.ca.gov) to file claims.

- Save documents in a dedicated "UI" folder.

- Screenshot job search logs.

- If English isn't your first language, use translated UI forms on www.dol.gov or call 211 for interpreters.

- Check www.dol.gov for state-specific rules and benefit details.

- Find free legal help at www.lsc.gov/find-legal-aid.

- Check www.unemploymentbenefitsguide.com for state-specific guides.

- Contact www.nlg.org for fraud or overpayment disputes.

- Some states now cover gig workers—verify eligibility at www.dol.gov.

- UI rules differ by state—know yours before you apply.

Chapter 24: Child Support — How the System Traps Everyone (Payers, Recipients, and Kids)

It's Supposed to Help Families. It Usually Hurts Them Instead.

Child support laws were meant to make sure kids didn't starve when parents split up.

What we got instead was a system that ruins families, wrecks credit, locks people up, and forces both sides into poverty.

This chapter breaks down how the child support system actually works and how it traps both the people paying and the people relying on it.

What Child Support Is (And Isn't)

- It's a court-ordered obligation.

- It's supposed to help the child.

- It's enforced by state agencies, with federal oversight under Title IV-D of the Social Security Act.

But:

- If the custodial parent receives TANF, the state may keep up to 50% of child support payments to offset TANF costs.

- Pass-through payments ($50–$200) vary by state; you may need to exit TANF to receive them—check www.acf.hhs.gov.

- Non-payment triggers punishment, not mediation.

- Child support is calculated using state formulas, often based on both parents' incomes, custody percentage, and child expenses like healthcare.

- It's often based on outdated income levels that don't adjust when life changes.

How the System Punishes Payers

Miss a payment? Here's what they can do:

- Garnish your wages (without notice).

- Seize your bank account.

- Suspend your driver's license (often if arrears exceed $2,500).

- Suspend professional licenses, hunting licenses, or fishing licenses, depending on the state.

- Take your tax refund.

- Report you to credit bureaus.

- Deny you a passport if arrears exceed $2,500—contact www.acf.hhs.gov for relief options.

- Jail you for contempt of court, but only after a hearing where they prove you're able but "unwilling" to pay. Unwilling being defined as liberally as needed.

None of these help a kid eat. Most just make it harder for the non-custodial parent to work, earn, or even travel to see their child.

How It Hurts Custodial Parents Too

The person raising the child often gets hit from both sides:

- If they receive TANF or state aid, the state may seize the child support and pocket it.

- Custodial parents on TANF may request exemptions to receive full support—ask your caseworker.

- If the paying parent falls behind, enforcement usually comes too late to actually help.

- Family courts rarely enforce visitation, even when tied to support orders.

Instead of security, many custodial parents get stuck chasing money through broken systems that punish both parents but help neither.

Why the System Doesn't Adjust for Reality

Child support amounts are set based on your income at the time of the order.

Lost your job? Got sick? Laid off?

- They don't automatically adjust.

- You have to go back to court and ask for a modification— and most people don't know that.

- To modify support, you must prove changed circumstances like job loss or illness.

- Modifications only apply forward; arrears still accrue until you file—act quickly.

- Meanwhile, debt piles up and triggers enforcement actions.

It's a system that assumes you're lying even when you're broke.

How to Avoid the Worst Traps

1. Get a formal modification as soon as your income changes.

- Many courts allow pro se (self-filed) motions.

2. Always document your payments.

- Pay by check, money order, or a state-monitored system. Never cash.

3. Don't ignore court notices.

- Missing court can trigger default judgments and arrest warrants.

4. If you're the custodial parent, check if the state is taking part of the payment.

- You may qualify for more if you're off TANF.

When It's Weaponized in Custody Fights

- Some parents use child support as leverage in custody or visitation disputes.

- The system rarely intervenes. It's seen as a civil issue.

- Some states mandate mediation for custody disputes— check www.nolo.com for local rules.

- Some courts waive mediation fees for low-income parents —check www.mediate.com.

145

- You can request court-ordered mediation, but enforcement is weak.

If you're in this situation, document everything. Be the one asking for mediation or a hearing. Even if it feels useless, it builds a paper trail.

What Happens If You Go to Jail Over Child Support

Jail doesn't erase the debt. It adds to it.

You'll likely still owe:

- The full back support.

- Interest (often 6–12% annually).

- Court costs.

- Any enforcement fees.

Contempt hearings must give you notice and a chance to respond —demand this if jailed.

Jailing a parent often removes their ability to pay anything and destroys employment, housing, or family relationships in the process.

If jailed for contempt, contact www.lsc.gov/find-legal-aid to challenge the order.

What Happens If You Leave the State

Many parents attempt to escape enforcement by moving to another state. But under the Uniform Interstate Family Support Act (UIFSA), states can enforce child support orders across state lines and may cooperate to garnish wages, suspend licenses, or pursue contempt charges.

Under UIFSA, a new state can modify orders if both parents relocate—check www.acf.hhs.gov.

Final Word

Child support is supposed to help kids. But the system wasn't built for that.

It was built to claw back state aid money, punish poor parents, and crank out enforcement stats.

Whether you're paying, receiving, or trying to avoid the system altogether, just know how it works before it works you over.

And never assume fairness will show up on its own.

Resources That May Help

- Check www.acf.hhs.gov for child support program details.
- Find legal help at www.lsc.gov/find-legal-aid.
- Review family law guides at www.nolo.com.
- Search affordable mediation options at www.mediate.com.
- Some states reduce arrears for low-income payers—ask your local legal aid office.

Chapter 25: Tax Credits — The Money They Hope You Don't Claim

You Might Be Leaving Thousands on the Table Without Knowing It

If you have ever said, "I don't make enough to file taxes," this chapter is for you.

If you have ever worked under the table or filed a basic return and did not get much back, this chapter is also for you.

Tax credits are not charity. They are legal entitlements meant to reduce poverty. Most go unclaimed because the system ensures you do not hear about them.

Why You Should File Taxes Even With No Income

- Filing a return makes you eligible for refundable credits. This is money the government pays you even if you owe nothing.

- It starts a three-year window for audits, refunds, and statute of limitations.

- It protects you if someone else tries to steal your identity and claim your credits.

- You can get an IRS Identity Protection PIN at www.irs.gov/ippin to prevent tax identity theft.

Even if you made zero dollars, file. Especially if you have children.

The Three Big Federal Credits You Might Qualify For

1. Earned Income Tax Credit (EITC)

- For low- and moderate-income workers.

- Can be worth up to approximately $7,500 depending on income and number of children.

- Some part-time workers qualify if they meet income thresholds.

- EITC income limits adjust yearly. For example, around $18,000 for single filers with no children and up to $64,000 with three or more children. Check www.irs.gov for current amounts.

You must file to receive the EITC. The IRS will not send it automatically.

2. Child Tax Credit (CTC)

- Up to $2,100 per child in 2025.

- Up to $1,600 of that amount may be refundable if your income is low.

- No advance payments are available after the pandemic programs ended.

You must file a tax return to claim it.

3. American Opportunity Tax Credit (AOTC)

- For students in their first four years of college.

- Worth up to $2,500 per year.

- Up to $1,000 is refundable even if you owe nothing.

- The credit covers tuition and required books but not room and board. Save receipts for proof.

Other Credits People Miss

- **Saver's Credit:** Up to $1,000 for singles or $2,000 for joint filers contributing to retirement accounts. Generally for incomes under approximately $38,000 (single) or $76,000 (joint).
- **Premium Tax Credit:** Available if you bought health insurance through a government marketplace.
- **Dependent Care Credit:** If you paid for childcare while working or looking for work.

State Credits Are Real and Often Forgotten

Many states offer:

- State-level Earned Income Tax Credits.
- Renters' credits.
- Property tax refunds.
- Childcare credits.

State credits vary widely. For example, state EITCs range from three to fifty percent of the federal EITC. Check www.taxcreditsforworkersandfamilies.org for details.

Where the System Works Against You

- Tax preparation chains take large cuts of refunds through

refund anticipation loans, which often charge twenty to forty percent fees.

- Commercial providers bury IRS Free File links and push paid services.

- IRS letters about credits often arrive months after you miss deadlines.

Where to File Without Paying a Dime

- **IRS Free File (for incomes under $79,000):** www.irs.gov/freefile.

- **GetYourRefund.org:** A nonprofit service offering free virtual tax preparation for low- and moderate-income filers.

- **VITA (Volunteer Income Tax Assistance):** Free in-person help for incomes under approximately $60,000. Find sites at www.irs.gov/vita.

Beware of tax preparation scams that charge for free services. Use only www.irs.gov/freefile, GetYourRefund.org, or VITA.

Final Word

If you are struggling financially, taxes may feel like a threat. However, tax credits remain one of the few direct cash systems in the United States that actually work if you know how to claim them.

Do not leave your money in the government's pocket.

File your return. Claim your credits. Take what is legally yours.

Additional Resources

- For tax credit details and updates, visit www.irs.gov.

- For state credit information, check www.taxcreditsforworkersandfamilies.org.

- For legal help with tax disputes, visit www.lsc.gov/find-legal-aid.

- To prevent tax identity theft, visit www.irs.gov/ippin.

- For mental health support related to financial stress, visit www.crisistextline.org.

- To keep up with digital filing trends, use www.irs.gov/freefile or your state tax portal.

- Check www.taxcreditsforworkersandfamilies.org for state credit expansions.

Tax credit amounts adjust annually for inflation. Expect higher limits in 2025. Always check www.irs.gov for the latest figures.

Chapter 26: Public School Rights — What They Won't Tell You About Enrollment, Meals, and Homeless Students

School Systems Rely on You Not Knowing the Rules

Most families do not realize how many rights they have inside the public school system or how often schools break the law by pretending you do not.

This chapter explains how to get your child enrolled, what to do if you are homeless or displaced, and how to ensure your child receives the services and meals they are entitled to without being shamed, blocked, or pushed out.

You Have the Right to Enroll Your Child Even If:

- You do not have permanent housing.

- You do not have all their paperwork.

- You do not have custody papers finalized.

- You do not have a utility bill or lease.

Under federal law (McKinney-Vento Act):

- Schools must enroll children immediately, even if documents are missing.

- Schools must assist you in obtaining missing records, such as birth certificates or immunizations.

- Schools must allow your child to remain in their school of origin, meaning the school they attended when stably housed or before displacement, when possible.

If You Are Homeless or Displaced (Even Temporarily):

You qualify for McKinney-Vento protections if you are:

- Couch surfing.

- In a shelter.

- Living in a motel or car.

- Doubled up with another family temporarily.

- A foster youth.

Your child can:

- Remain in their original school.

- Receive transportation assistance.

- Enroll immediately in a new school.

- Receive free meals automatically.

Every school must have a McKinney-Vento liaison — a designated person responsible for assisting families in this situation. Ask for them by name.

Free and Reduced Lunch: You Do Not Have to Starve to Qualify

- Any child in a household under specific income limits qualifies.

- Children in households receiving SNAP, TANF, or McKinney-Vento protections automatically qualify for free meals.

- Schools cannot single out or shame students over unpaid meal debts.

- Some states offer free lunch to all students. As of 2025, more than eight states provide universal free lunch. Check with your local school district or visit www.fns.usda.gov.

- Free lunch eligibility applies if household income is under approximately $39,000 for a family of four in 2025.

Special Education and Services

If your child has learning differences or disabilities:

- You have the right to request an evaluation at any time.

- Schools cannot refuse or delay once you request in writing.

- Schools must evaluate within sixty days of your written request.

- You may appeal or request an independent evaluation if you disagree with the school's findings.

- Schools must provide services under the Individuals with Disabilities Education Act (IDEA), regardless of budget constraints.

- Schools may delay IDEA evaluations due to staffing shortages. Demand written timelines and escalate concerns to www.ed.gov/ocr.

How Schools Intimidate Parents

Schools often try to discourage families by claiming:

- "We cannot enroll your child without this document."
- "We are out of space."
- "We do not offer those services here."
- "You have to wait until the next semester."
- "You must prove residency."

These are illegal stalling tactics.

Document every interaction. Ask for everything in writing. Request the McKinney-Vento liaison or the special education coordinator when necessary.

What To Say When They Push Back

- "I am requesting immediate enrollment under McKinney-Vento."
- "I am requesting an evaluation under IDEA."
- "I am requesting this in writing."

If the school continues to stall, escalate your concerns to:

- The district superintendent.
- The school board.
- The state education ombudsman.
- The U.S. Department of Education's Office for Civil Rights at www.ed.gov/ocr.

Final Word

Public schools are supposed to be the last guaranteed service available in America. Yet, many still try to gatekeep, delay, or deny services unless you assert your rights.

Do not ask permission to protect your child. Demand it.

The law is already on your side.

Additional Resources

- For homeless student resources, visit www.ed.gov/mckinney-vento.

- For school meal program details, visit www.fns.usda.gov.

- For special education support, visit www.parentcenterhub.org.

- For IDEA disputes, visit www.ed.gov/ocr.

- For mental health support related to advocacy stress, visit www.crisistextline.org.

- Many schools now require online enrollment. Ask for paper options if needed.

- Family homelessness increased by fifteen percent in 2024. McKinney-Vento protections are critical.

- School disputes can be stressful for families. Use support resources to stay informed and strong.

Chapter 27: Immigration Status and Access to Benefits — What You Can Get (Even If They Say You Can't)

They Count on You Assuming You Have No Rights

Immigrants, whether documented or undocumented, are often shut out of benefits, housing, jobs, and services. Much of the time, this exclusion is illegal.

This chapter explains which benefits you may qualify for, how mixed-status families are treated, and how to protect yourself from illegal denials and intimidation.

First Rule: They Cannot Deny You Basic Public Services Based on Immigration Alone

In the United States, regardless of your immigration status, you have the right to:

- Attend public schools. The Supreme Court's decision in Plyler v. Doe guarantees access to K-12 education.

- Use hospital emergency rooms for medical care. Emergency Medicaid covers childbirth, life-threatening conditions, and acute injuries. It does not cover routine care.

- Get vaccinated at public health clinics.

- Access emergency shelters. Some shelters may request identification but cannot deny services based on immigration status.

- Use food pantries and most church-run services.

These rights are protected by federal laws, court decisions, and constitutional guarantees.

Benefits You May Still Qualify For Even Without Legal Status

- **WIC (Women, Infants, and Children Program):** No citizenship requirement. You must provide proof of state residency, such as a utility bill.

- **Emergency Medicaid:** Covers emergency care, childbirth, and life-threatening conditions.

- **Local and State Aid:** Some states, like California and New York, provide housing, food, or healthcare assistance regardless of immigration status. Examples include California's Medi-Cal and New York's Emergency Rental Assistance Program. Check local programs.

- **Legal Aid:** Most legal aid clinics assist with housing, labor rights, and certain civil cases, regardless of immigration status.

If You Have a Mixed-Status Family (Some Citizens, Some Not)

- U.S.-born children are eligible for SNAP, Medicaid, and TANF.

- The household may still qualify for assistance even if the parents are undocumented.

- Household income from undocumented parents may count

when applying, but families cannot be denied solely because of the parents' status.

- You are not required to provide a Social Security Number for household members who are not applying for benefits.

Public Charge: What It Actually Means

- Public charge rules apply only to people applying for green cards or visas.

- Only certain benefits count toward public charge determinations.

- Benefits like SNAP, WIC, Medicaid for children, housing aid, and pandemic relief generally do not count.

- Public charge policies can shift with new administrations. Always check www.uscis.gov/public-charge for current guidelines.

If anyone tries to use "public charge" warnings to scare you, seek legal advice before giving up a benefit you may need.

What They Cannot Do But Often Try Anyway

- Deny school enrollment based on citizenship status.

- Deny emergency medical care.

- Demand proof of immigration status for WIC or emergency assistance.

- Threaten you with ICE for seeking legal services.

Reporting ICE threats is protected. Report concerns to

www.nilc.org confidentially.

If You Get Threatened or Denied

- Ask for the policy in writing.

- Document every interaction.

- Contact local immigrant rights organizations or a legal aid office.

- Use a trusted advocate or representative when dealing with agencies.

Final Word

The immigration system may be harsh, but most public services in the United States are governed by laws that protect you.

Do not assume you have no rights because of your immigration status.

Many times, when someone says "you do not qualify," they are counting on you to believe it without question.

Get help. Learn your rights. Do not let fear shut you out.

Additional Resources

- For public charge guidelines, visit www.uscis.gov/public-charge.

- For legal aid, visit www.lsc.gov/find-legal-aid.

- For immigrant rights, visit www.nilc.org.

- For mental health support, visit www.crisistextline.org.

- For local community services, check trusted immigrant advocacy groups in your area.

- For California's Medi-Cal information, visit www.dhcs.ca.gov.

- If facing digital barriers, ask agencies for paper forms or in-person options.

Family homelessness, intimidation tactics, and digital-only application systems are all on the rise. Stay informed. Assert your rights. Seek support before giving up your access to help.

Chapter 28: You're Not Powerless

You Were Just Never Meant to Know the Rules

The system did not break. It was built this way.

You were never supposed to know how to appeal. You were never supposed to know how to demand that they put it in writing. You were never supposed to know how to get a judge to hear you, how to file before you were ready, how to build a paper trail, or how to hold your ground when they tried to wear you down.

They counted on you being too tired. They counted on you feeling too humiliated. They counted on you standing alone.

This book is not a magic fix. It will not erase your debt. It will not force the courts to listen. It will not change the system overnight. But it gives you the one thing you have been missing — a real map of how the game is played.

Once you see it, you cannot unsee it.

What You Have Now

- You know how to apply for the help you are entitled to — and how they will try to make you quit before you get it.

- You know how to push back when they stall, deny, or lie.

- You know how the courts, police, and agencies feed on your fear and confusion.

- You know your rights in schools, shelters, courts, and every system that touches your life — and how to use them.

- You know how to protect your privacy, safeguard your

family, and defend your freedom.

- You know how to build your own safety nets when the system leaves you hanging.

This is not the end of your fight. It is the end of fighting blind.

You do not have to be wealthy. You do not have to be powerful. You do not have to be fearless.

You only have to know how not to fold when the system plays its game. And now you do.

Final Word

You were never the problem.

You have been playing a game rigged to make you believe you could not win.

Now you know better.

Stay informed. Stay organized. Stand your ground.

Because you are not powerless — you were just never supposed to learn the rules.

Your Next Steps

- Review the chapters when you need a refresher.
- Reach out for legal help when facing threats or intimidation.
- Document everything. Keep records even when it feels like overkill.
- Share this knowledge with others who need it.
- Never accept "no" as the final answer until you check for

yourself.

You have a right to stand your ground. You have a right to know the rules.

And now, you do.

ABOUT THE AUTHOR

James Ergle writes for people who know something's broken and want more than slogans. He's a political essayist and private investigator who's spent years inside the systems he now critiques.

His Substack, <u>Radical Leanings</u>, combines essays, political cartoons, and structural breakdowns for readers who want to understand how power really works and how it might be replaced. He writes like someone explaining the world to his younger self, and thousands of readers have joined him for that reason.

This is his fifth book.

www.ingramcontent.com/pod-product-compliance
Lightning Source LLC
Chambersburg PA
CBHW052020030426
42335CB00026B/3215